BEST METHODS
OF STUDY

About the Authors

Samuel Smith received the degrees of A.M. and Ph.D. from New York University. He has held positions as research assistant for the New York State Board of Regents' Inquiry into the Character and Cost of Public Education; supervisor and director of research for government programs of adult education; research director and co-author of the National Achievement Tests; and editor of the Dryden Press Handbooks of Physics, Psychology, Educational Psychology, and Sociology. Dr. Smith is co-author of *Supervision in the Elementary School* and *Education and Society* and a contributor to *Principles of Sociology* and *Educational Psychology* in the College Outline Series. He is currently head of the Editorial Department of Barnes and Noble, Inc.

Louis Shores did his undergraduate work at Toledo University, received his M.S. at the College of the City of New York, and his Ph.D. at Peabody College for Teachers in Nashville, Tennessee. From 1933 to 1946 he was Librarian and Director of the Library School at Peabody College. Since 1946 he has been Dean of the Library School at Florida State University in Tallahassee. Dean Shores is an associate editor of *Collier's Encyclopedia*. Among the many books he has written are: *Highways in the Sky; Origins of the American College Library; Bibliographies and Summaries in Education; Basic Reference Sources.*

Robert Brittain received the degrees of A. M. and Ph.D. from Princeton University. He has taught at Texas Technical College, Ohio State University, and Queens College, where he was an assistant professor in the English Department. During 1945-1946 he taught at the United States Army University in France. Dr. Brittain is the author of *Punctuation, Poems by Christopher Smart,* and *Let There Be Bread.*

BEST METHODS OF STUDY

Samuel Smith

With Special Sections By

Louis Shores

Robert Brittain

BARNES & NOBLE, Inc. • NEW YORK

Publishers • Booksellers • Since 1873

Preface

Most books on methods of study have stressed general ideals and theories. Few indeed are the texts which provide the student with practical helps. For the college freshman or high-school senior, this volume presents a brief summary of suggestions applicable to his immediate needs. The authors believe that a more extensive book might be desirable. As at present organized, however, colleges and secondary schools, with rare exceptions, could not make practical use of a highly detailed or elaborate treatise in this field. The authors have, therefore, endeavored chiefly to answer the student's urgent questions, What shall I do? and How shall I do it? For the most part, only important points have been included.

In colleges and senior high-schools, not enough emphasis has been placed on the mastery of the best methods of study. This shortcoming probably accounts for the results of a recent poll taken at one of the large eastern universities. Of three hundred and twenty seniors in the poll, more than one-third admitted they did not know how to study. To make the challenge even more pointed, two-thirds of the same group of three hundred and twenty seniors stated they required special tutoring for examinations. Such unfortunate conditions are by no means uncommon. They demonstrate effectively the need of a brief summary to help the student achieve all the success of which he is capable.

The book may be used either as a text for systematic courses or as a reference book applicable to the various major subjects and activities of the curriculum. Students should be encouraged to discuss the suggestions offered, and to test the merits of recommendations by trying them out in practice.

Acknowledgments

Acknowledgments are gratefully made to the following authorities: Dr. Robert Brittain, for contributing the Chapter on Punctuation; Dr. Louis Shores, Dean of the Library School at Florida State University, for the Chapter on the Library and Reference Works: and to Mr. Edward Fitzgerald for planning and revising the Chapter on Visual Aids. The following educators supplied helpful criticisms of the original manuscript: Professor C. C. Crawford, of the University of Southern California; Professor Robert A. Davis, formerly of the University of Colorado; the late Professor Herman Harrell Horne, of New York University; Professor John C. Snidecor, formerly of the University of Idaho; and Professor Paul V. West, Emeritus, of New York University.

The authors wish also to acknowledge many practical suggestions received from the following authorities who read the page proofs: Marie Y. Andrews, Dean, Mansfield (Pa.) State Teachers College; Dorothy McSparran Arnold, Dean, New York University; Adelaide P. Bostick, Dean, Boiling Springs Junior College; Mary Rogers Brown, Dean, Arkansas State College; E. Alverna Burdick, Dean, Connecticut College; Susan B. Davis, Dean, University of Wisconsin; Dora K. Degen, Dean, Alfred University; Olivia N. Dorman, Dean, Florida State College for Women; Helen F. Faust, Dean, Pennsylvania State College; R. Louise Fitch, Dean, Cornell University; Mildred P. French, Dean, Connecticut State College; Dorothy Gebauer, Dean, University of Texas; Helen M. Hosp, Dean, Bethany College; Eleanor Kitchin, Dean, Boston University; Mary B. Merritt, Dean, University of Miami; Helen E. Peck, Dean, Rhode Island State College; Sister Marie St.

Eleanor, Dean, University of Dayton; Lucy Ward Stebbins, Dean, University of California; Professor George S. Wills, Western Maryland College; Edith G. Wilson, Dean, University of Maine; and Professor George B. Woods, American University.

The reactions of many students who read copies of a preliminary draft of the manuscript helped the authors in their final selection of material for the book. It is not possible to list the names of all these students, but for generous aid the authors wish to express special gratitude to Laurence Dalcher, Derna DePamphilis, and Yole Granata.

Table of Contents

Table of Contents

x

Table of Contents

CHAPTER ONE

The Importance of
EFFICIENCY

> "To be strenuous is to put forth greater effort; to be efficient is to put forth less effort. . . . Efficiency brings about greater results with lessened effort; strenuousness brings about greater results with abnormally greater effort."—Harrington Emerson*

Why does one individual learn more quickly and thoroughly than another? The chief reasons for inefficiency in learning are carelessness and ineffective habits of study. In many cases, observance of a few important rules would insure success. Let us assume that you require ordinarily about ninety hours to master the important elements of a new subject. Would you not like to achieve the same results in sixty hours instead of ninety? Investigations have shown that most students can save from one-fourth to one-third of their time if they systematize their efforts in accordance with the chief principles of learning.

Speed is not the only advantage of proper study methods. Effective methods help the student understand and remember what he is studying. Most of the educational handicaps of individuals are caused by failure to study in the best possible way. Many hours of needless anxiety might be avoided through knowledge of a few practical suggestions. You may be more gifted in

---

* From, *The Twelve Principles of Efficiency* by Harrington Emerson. Used by permission of the publishers, McGraw-Hill Book Co., New York.

studying one subject than in studying another, but the correct application of your efforts will increase your enjoyment and success in all fields of education.

Consider a concrete example. You may read a chapter of a textbook several times, and still get very little out of it. On the other hand, you may read it only once or twice, and get a great deal out of it. In the latter case, the chances are that you followed certain practical rules of study; perhaps, you criticized, compared, digested, asked questions, found questions and answers, or applied some of the other procedures of efficient learning. It is, in fact, easier to study in the right way than it is to use wasteful or partly successful methods.

Everyone who needs to do so can improve his habits of study. It is, however, necessary to discover one's most urgent requirements. Perhaps you need to perfect your use of reference materials, or your methods of reading. Perhaps you are not aware of the most helpful hints for studying a particular subject. Useful principles and devices may be suggested. The conscientious application of energy is indispensable. Learning how to study should make your efforts more direct and effective. But you must select the hints that will be of greatest assistance in your situation. Are you reading quickly, with good retention? Is your mastery of subject-matter complete, well balanced? Have you weak spots in special subjects? Find your handicaps; refer to study helps relating to these handicaps; and apply useful hints to your daily practices.

Do not be satisfied with partial success. You can, and should, learn all subjects you study, learn them quickly, master them thoroughly, and achieve a record of all-round ability. Enough time should remain for hobbies, social activities, exploratory reading, and other constructive experiences. The successful student's first care is, however, for the efficient completion of all educational tasks. Efficiency means doing things on time, thoroughly, in the best possible way, in the one way that is best for you. To maintain such efficiency, you should check up on your daily habits of study, plan ahead, and select useful suggestions for experimental application. *Systematic methods of learning may require more effort and patience in the beginning; but soon, they become habitual and effective.*

A few simple suggestions may increase your efficiency considerably. (1) Make up a schedule for your studying. Discipline yourself to follow your schedule, and be sure that you allow enough time for each subject. (2) Set aside a suitable place for your work and begin promptly. (3) Concentrate until you have finished at least one major worthwhile task. (4) Keep up with your daily assignments; better still, do more than is required. (5) Limit your program and everyday efforts to what you can accomplish, bearing in mind that it is better to learn one or two topics thoroughly than four or five topics inaccurately or superficially. (6) Instead of worrying about examinations and personal problems, keep busy. Since worrying and daydreaming are futile and merely waste valuable time, take constructive action to meet each problem, do your best, and make the best of the consequences.

CHAPTER TWO

READING

> "Some great men—Gibbon was one and
> Daniel Webster was another and the great
> Lord Stafford was a third—always, before
> reading a book, made a short, rough analysis
> of the questions which they expected to be
> answered in it, the additions to be made to
> their knowledge, and whither it would take
> them. I have sometimes tried that way of
> studying, and guiding attention; I have
> never done so without advantage, and I com-
> mend it to you."—John Morley

Main Types of Reading. The three main types of
reading are: (1) the quick-reference type, to obtain information, to answer questions, or to follow directions;
(2) the study type (critical reading), to master ideas and
to organize, interpret, and evaluate facts; and (3) the
aesthetic type (recreational reading), to derive enjoyment and appreciation. This chapter offers suggestions
to improve efficiency in these three main types of reading.

Preparation. The first step is to form the habit of
making adequate preparation. Develop a plan or system. Decide carefully what to read and for what purposes. If you wish to read only parts of a book, choose
them wisely, for some books cannot be read efficiently
in "bits and patches." Frequently, in well-organized
books, the precise meaning depends on preceding sections.

Consider the following preliminary questions: Is the
material worth much of your time, or should you merely
skim through it? What questions do you expect the book
to explain or answer? What did the author have in mind,
and for whom did he prepare the material? Should you
read it immediately or later? What prejudices or con-

4

victions have you formed about the subject? Read a few paragraphs aloud to ascertain the author's attitude and style. Anticipate difficulties you may encounter in reading his work. Set aside enough time, and discipline yourself to avoid distractions.

Efficiency in Reading. Two main factors in efficiency are speed and comprehension. Since both are involved in reading any kind of subject-matter, it is impossible to measure them independently of each other. Recent experiments have shown that it is much easier to increase one's rate of reading than it is to improve one's power to comprehend. The following paragraphs suggest ways to increase reading speed. The remaining paragraphs discuss methods of improving comprehension.

Speed of Reading. As a rule, outstanding students are quick readers. Speed is important, for it permits you to cover more ground or to review the same materials repeatedly within a limited period of time. Probably the best rule for the development of speed in reading is to practice, with the deliberate purpose of increasing your speed.

Some readers read too slowly because of faulty, correctible habits or environmental conditions, such as the following:

1. Failure to bear in mind definite purposes for reading.

2. Inadequate preparation.

3. Bad posture, poor lighting, or other environmental deficiencies.

4. Defective vision, which might be ameliorated or corrected.

5. Excessive lip movements. The eye can move much faster than lip and throat muscles.

6. Regressive movements caused by lack of concentration or of comprehension.

7. Excessive attention to single words (or parts of words) instead of word groups. (Conversely, failure to

note minor words which change the entire meaning of a sentence.)

8. Failure to connect different parts of reading material with each other. The whole story of a chapter or a book should be considered frequently during the reading of any section.

9. Excessive guesswork as to the precise meaning of words.

10. Failure to concentrate on the central thoughts and significant supporting details. (Conversely, failure to pause for rest or reflection may affect speed and comprehension adversely.)

Speed of reading is less important with subject-matter that requires much reflection or analysis than it is with material that is mainly informational in character. A slow pace is usually necessary when studying a difficult text. Even in such cases, however, a quick overview, by skimming rapidly through a chapter, may be highly desirable before you begin slow reading of the chapter. Use good judgment in adapting speed to the kind of book you are reading. It would be foolhardy to dash through one of Shakespeare's plays a few times, and call it a day. This type of subject-matter requires you to review difficult sections, ask questions about what you read, think intensively about language, style, characters, structure, and so on. Develop the ability to read at a high speed; but use the ability wisely, to insure the degree of mastery you wish to acquire.

Reviews. Analyze a topic before reading about it. Benefit from your past experience. Learning is much like the construction of a house on a solid foundation; and every useful idea you can think of will serve as another basis for clear understanding of what you read. The words of a text would be meaningless to you if you had not seen them in similar context before, or if you could not explain them in terms of words you have used in the past. In like manner, a quick review of your knowledge about a topic will help you master new ideas and facts. A student beginning the study of modern European history might do well to skim through the main events and trends of medieval history. Reviews should not be overdone; consider carefully how much you should undertake when you begin to study new material.

On the other hand, when studying material requiring thorough mastery, you should resist the temptation to be satisfied with quick reading and casual reflection. Perhaps you have understood the chief ideas of an author, and painstaking review does not seem attractive. But remember that superficial reading of a textbook does not mean that you will remember its important points. You must take time to think seriously about those points. True, there are books through which you may wish only to glance. *But be sure that you do not mistake skimming for thorough study.* For the latter, careful re-reading is necessary, together with comparisons and contrasts, critical reactions, analysis of implications, questions and answers.

Careful Study. Summarize what you read. Re-state the ideas in your own words. Put a whole chapter in a nutshell of a few sentences. You will then possess a new center of reference for further study of the same or related materials. Digest; consider the relative importance of items; associate details with major points; build a unified picture of the subject-matter as a whole. Go over the parts you like best; and criticize the parts you dislike. A quick final re-reading may be helpful.

Self-Correction. It is often a good idea to test yourself on what you have been reading. Ask yourself questions, and refer to the text to verify your answers. The best students generally stop reading, from time to time, to test themselves on what they have read. Whenever they find they have forgotten vital points, they study more carefully. They find and correct mistakes they have made in their interpretation of the text.

Memory. If you wish to remember the ideas in a book, you must understand them clearly and associate them with each other and with other ideas. Often, real understanding requires background reading about the topics being studied. Be sure that you understand the first steps thoroughly, for, in many subjects, the more advanced material depends upon what has preceded it. Bear in mind the following useful suggestions by Dr. James D. Weinland, the noted psychologist, for remembering any important fact: "(1) Try to see its significance, try to be interested in it . . . (2) Give it your attention, be sure you have it right. (3) Be sure you fully understand it. (4) Intend to remember it. (5) Be confident that you can remember it. (6) Involve the ego, if possible. (7) Associate it with other related facts. (8) Fix it in its proper place in your memory system. (9) See it as part of a larger whole. (10) If there is a basis for doing so, learn it as part of a small group of related facts."*

Persistence. You cannot expect everything you study to be chock full of interest and drama. To achieve results that are interesting and important, you may have to read a certain amount of material that is dull, uninspiring, perhaps even poorly written. Try to inject life into such topics; connect them, if you can, with more attractive subject-matter. The chances are that as you proceed to master one section after another, the task will become tolerable if not really pleasant.

---

* From *How to Improve Your Memory* by James D. Weinland (in *Everyday Handbook Series*), published by Barnes and Noble, Inc., 1957.

Mechanics of Reading. There are a few points to consider regarding the mechanics of reading. Titles and topical headings give you a key to the main ideas of a text; if there are no topical headings, construct them for yourself. The professional standing of the author may also be of importance. Has he written a great deal? Has he changed his ideas? Does his record show reliability? Would you expect him to be partisan in point of view? When, and under what circumstances, was the text written? Note the full name of the author and the latest copyright date. It is the copyright date, usually placed on the reverse side of the title page, which is important to remember, not the printing date sometimes included on the title page. In the preface, if there be one, note the reasons given for writing the volume, and suggestions on how best to use it. Be sure you have a good idea of the complete plan of the author. Consult the table of contents. After you have read a book, try to discover the reasons why certain chapters were placed first and others last.

The Introduction. The introduction is an important part of nearly every book. Here, the author generally introduces you more directly to the subject-matter of the volume. He gives you an idea of his general point of view. When reading the introduction, try to answer questions such as these: What are the chief assumptions in the introduction? To what extent are they justified? Does the style of the introduction indicate labored writing that will require slow reading and careful weighing of terms? Would it be best to consult simpler works before studying this text?

Adequate consideration of the introduction should help you decide the best way to use the book, and how much you may expect to get out of it.

If there is a preface as well as an introduction, the introduction generally follows the preface. Figures 1 and 2 are illustrations of these two sections of a textbook.

**PARAGRAPH
DISCUSSES:**

Authors
Scope
Approach
Application

Materials
Application
Attitude of
Authors
Content

New material
Scope

To whom volume
is addressed
Instructions

PREFACE TO REVISED EDITION

This outline, constructed by a group of specialists, each an acknowledged expert in the topic assigned to him, presents the most important and practical essentials of educational psychology. The essentials are submitted not from any one point of view, but from the diversified views of various schools of thought. Problems and conclusions are based upon many years of experience in the preparation of teachers, and critical analyses of recent developments in the science of psychology. The outline as a whole comprises a bird's eye view, though an adequately complete picture, of practical facts applicable to teaching and learning situations.

The authors have analyzed major factors and theories as expounded in the popular textbooks in this field. Students of education will, therefore, find the presentation admirably suited to their needs, regardless of the particular textbooks they may possess. All sections of the outline were written in accordance with an impartial scientific spirit. They reflect well balanced maturity of vision, and embody not only logically arranged standard subject matter, but also invaluable creative contributions.

This revised edition also contains analyses of recent developments in educational psychology. Several new volumes have been added as basic sources and a comprehensive bibliography has been included. The major concepts, facts, and references presented in *fifteen* standard textbooks have thus been made available, together with a synopsis of contemporary theories and data.

Although intended primarily for students and teachers, the volume contains information of great interest to parents and others concerned with educational problems. Each section is preceded by a page listing the main topics analyzed. It is recommended that the reader refer to each of these topics in turn; and that he question his knowledge of the topic, both before and after reading its summary.

S. S.

New York City
November, 1935

Fig. 1. Note the marginal headings indicating the nature of the materials included in a typical preface such as the above.

Note the differences in content between the preface and the introduction.

The Index. As you read, refer to the index to get more ideas about a point you are reading. One topic will suggest another: find and criticize the author's treatment of these topics. You may have to look under several headings, in the index, to find the subject-matter in which you are interested. As a rule, numbers in

INTRODUCTION

THE SCIENCE OF EDUCATIONAL PSYCHOLOGY

By

SAMUEL SMITH

A. Scientific Method and Educational Psychology

1. Genesis of Scientific Method.

In primitive society inquiry concerning the phenomena of nature was restricted largely to uncritical traditions and superstitions. *Ancient religions*, however, developed systematic beliefs as to the meaning and structure of the universe. The wonder, fear, and hope of mankind found a welcome measure of security and satisfaction in the growth of religious solutions and faiths. Soon the curiosity of man proved flexible and insatiable. In·response to the demands of an inquisitive human intellect, Greek thinkers organized a non-religious type of reasoning or orderly speculation, called *philosophy*. The genesis of psychology represented a logical step from critical analysis of man's place in the world to a more detailed and painstaking investigation of his characteristics. The science of psychology has, therefore, sprung from the roots of classical philosophy. Early philosophers were, in fact, the predecessors and often the founders of physical, biological, and social methods and branches of research. Philosophers such as Aristotle utilized two general methods of inquiry, to wit: the logical-deductive, deducing facts from general principles, and the inductive-scientific, arriving at general principles by analysis of specific facts. But the works of Aristotle proved so profoundly impressive, clear, and logical that his major convictions were for centuries accepted as authoritative and irrefutable. The fact was ignored that Aristotle himself believed in and practiced the scientific procedures of observation and experimentation.

2. Characteristics of Science.

Leaders of the modern scientific trend, such as Francis Bacon (1561-1626), Galileo (1564-1642), Rene Descartes (1596-1650), Isaac Newton (1642-1727), John Locke (1632-1704), and Auguste Comte (1798-1857) reverted to Aristotle's inductive method; demanded experimental proofs; and insisted on empirical evidence as

3

FIG. 2.   This introduction, part of which is reproduced above, is concluded on additional pages with discussions of (3) Science of Psychology; (4) Methods of Psychological Research; (5) Principles of Research in Educational Psychology; (6) Nature of Educational Psychology; (7, 8, 9) Problems, Schools, and Contributions of Educational Psychology.

indexes refer to pages; but in some instances, they designate paragraphs or other parts of the volume. In the index, below, note the brief explanation of symbols and the significance of bold type.

Illustrations, Charts, Maps, Diagrams, etc. The importance of visual aids cannot be over-emphasized. Pages of tedious description may often be more effectively expressed in a single picture, graph, or map.

Modern authors rarely overlook an opportunity to use these devices when writing text and reference books. It is, therefore, to your advantage to learn how to interpret quickly and accurately, the wealth of information concentrated in carefully constructed illustrative materials. Types and functions of visual aids are further discussed in Chapter XVII.

References and Questions. Be sure you read all references and footnotes in the textbook. Instead of glancing at such references, question their importance, and write down at once the names of books to which you should refer.

Answer every important question in the text. If you are doubtful as to the correct reply, write the answer, then look up the problem in one of the references suggested by the author. Compare your answers with those which he has given.

If the text has indicated which references or questions are most significant (through bold-type headings or asterisks), concentrate on these; but if there is no indication of this kind, glance through the references and questions, and underline the most important ones.

You should know about several common methods of making references:

ibid.: this word means "the same," and refers you to the reference immediately preceding.

op. cit.: these words refer you to the last preceding citation, or reference, to the book of a particular author. For example, you may read "Professor John Jones" and find at the bottom of the page "op. cit. p. 12." You must then turn back in the footnotes until you find the reference to the book by Professor Jones; and you will there secure the title of his book. The page num-

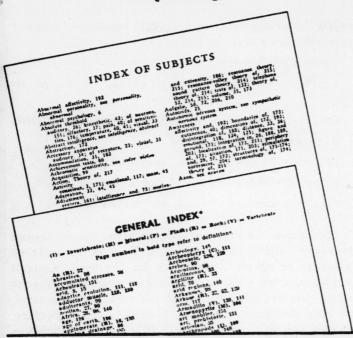

Fig. 3. Two types of indexes are reproduced above. Note that the bottom one not only refers to pages and points out definitions by the use of bold type, but also indicates the nature of each subject by inserting abbreviations.

ber after the words "op. cit." in this example, refers to the page in the volume written by Professor John Jones.

cf. p. 10: these abbreviations refer the reader to another page. They mean: consult page ten for further discussion of this or a related topic.

Some books have references at the end of a chapter, or at the end of the volume. You must then trace the numbers from the page you are reading to the reference. Before you read a book, consider the system of references and construct a plan for using them.

Other marks and abbreviations frequently used in books are as follows:

* † ¹ call attention to footnotes, usually in smaller type, at the bottom of the page.

§ usually indicates section.

e.g., from the Latin "exempli gratia," means *for example.*

etc., from the Latin "et cetera," means *and so forth.*

ff. means *following.*

i.e., from the Latin "id est," means *that is.*

p., pp., are abbreviations of *page* and *pages.*

viz., from the Latin "videlicet," means *namely.*

Glossaries. Certain textbooks present lists of special terms used, with their meanings. These words make up a glossary or special vocabulary for the text. Consult the glossary, as well as the index, whenever in your reading you are doubtful about the meaning of a term. You may also copy the terms included in the glossary, and test yourself occasionally. If you do not know a term thoroughly, look it up not only in the glossary and the index, but also in the text itself. If you are still a bit uncertain about the term, consult the dictionary, an encyclopedia, or one of the reference books suggested by the author of the book. Make practical use of the term; apply it in writing and discussion.

Appendixes. Supplementary materials of a statistical, explanatory, or informative nature are often placed at the end of the book, in appendixes. Review such materials carefully; they may prove to be of great value in your study of the subject.

Varieties of Type. These include the use of bold type, italics, capitals, Roman numerals (I, II, III, etc.), Arabic numerals (1, 2, 3, etc.), letters (A, B, C, a, b, c, etc.), and parentheses, ( ), or brackets, [ ]. Varieties

---

APPENDIX III

GLOSSARY*

Acetobacter (Gr.) Aerobic bacilli which secure their energy by the oxidation of alcohol to acetic acid.

Acetyl-methyl carbinol (Gr.) A keto-isomer of aldol formed from glucose by some bacteria and tested for by the Voges-Proskauer reaction. Ex.-Vibrio Cholera.

Actinobacillus (Gr.) A small rod belonging to the genus actinomyceteae.

Actinomyces (Gr.) Parasitic fungi with radiating mycelia and small spores.

Aerobic (Gr.) Requiring free oxygen for metabolism.

Aerogens (Gr.) Gas-producing bacteria.

Agglutination (Gr.) Clumping of bacteria in presence of type specific antiserum. (See somatic)

Fig. 4. Most textbooks of a technical nature include definitions of terms peculiar to the subject. Although fully discussed in the text, the meanings of these words are often included in a single section near the end of the book. Be sure you know the exact definitions of the words you use.

of type, and the spacing of the materials, give you an idea of the relative importance of different parts of a paragraph or section. They also help you discover connections among ideas.

The most important headings are generally printed in capitals or in bold type. Italics indicate significant points. The following arrangement is typical, in order of the importance of the subject-matter:

BOLD TYPE CAPITAL LETTERS

LARGE CAPITAL LETTERS

BOLD TYPE SMALL CAPITALS

Bold type, smaller sizes

Italics

Numerous variations of this order are possible. Become well acquainted with the system used in the particular text you are reading.

CHAPTER THREE

UNDERLINING

> "Now some folks dislike my use of my books in this way. They love their books so much that they think it nothing short of sacrilege to mark up a book. But to me that's like having a child so prettily dressed that you can't romp and play with it. What is the use of a good book, I say, if it is too pretty to use? I like to have my books speak to me, and then I like to talk back to them."
> —Phillips Brooks*

Purposes of Underlining. Underlining is useful for the following purposes:

1. To designate weak spots in mastery of subject-matter,

2. To indicate important problems, facts, and ideas to be considered and remembered,

3. To distinguish facts from opinions, and truths from errors,

4. To make a word, sentence, paragraph, idea, or argument easy to locate, and

5. To point out selected passages, words, or facts that will be needed for special uses, such as, to clinch an argument or to apply knowledge to practical affairs.

Points to Underline. *You may underline only in books that you own,* including your reference books, and in

---

* From *The Americanization of Edward Bok.*

notebooks. Often, it will help you to read your own notes if you underline the most important points. Proper underlining shows a degree of mastery and a sense of discrimination between what is basic and what is merely ornamental or supplementary. But you must use good judgment, avoid excessive underlining, weigh and consider before selecting key sentences, and adapt your action to the purpose you have in mind. Read or write a whole passage before underlining any part of it.

Underlining of Weak Spots. Use a red pencil. When you have learned a point thoroughly, go over the red line with a black pencil. You may do likewise with a whole chapter; if you are not sure you have mastered it, underscore the title in red; after sufficient review, mark it in black.

Underlining of Key Facts. It is not enough simply to underline the main points you want to remember. As you underline, and later as you review the subject-matter, supply from your imagination or memory the supplementary items that explain or enrich the chief ideas underlined. Be satisfied only when you have a complete, comprehensive, unified picture of the whole story. Fill in details, in your mind, and be sure to grasp the connections between one major point and the next.

Underlining of Doubtful Statements. Suppose you read a statement you disbelieve or cannot understand, or suppose you write about interesting ideas of which you are not quite sure. Opposite each questionable statement, place a question mark, preferably in the right-hand margin of the page. Underline these statements. Later, when you consult the underscored sections, you will know at once that the assertions are doubtful, puzzling, vague, or untrue. If, after further study, you find the material clear and accurate, mark a cross over the question mark, indicating that the statement is no longer open to doubt.

Underlining of Passages To Review. Decide whether you may ever want to review the subject-matter you are studying. If so, bear this possibility in mind when you underline. Select the points that will probably be important for the purpose of review. Use your pencil in moderation, but freely enough to help you regain the essence of the text, at a glance, should you return to it at a later date. With certain kinds of material, it may be a good idea to close the book now and then, and try to recall the content of the passages you have underlined.

Underlining of Special Passages. You may wish to indicate passages for which you expect to have an important practical need. Use the double line (═══════) in such cases. When underlining a textbook, list the double-lined pages on the inside cover page, for quick reference. Also designate very briefly, on the cover page, the general idea or use of the items listed.

Follow-Up Work on Underlined Sections. Properly used, underlining is an excellent aid to students. Be sure, however, to analyze the underlined sections; supply reactions to them; criticize, evaluate, apply your own ideas in some practical way; elaborate main points with details, imagination, and comparisons.

Example of Underlining. The following passages are underscored in accordance with the suggestions offered above.

 "Sociology may be divided into these subdivisions: "Social Problems, or what is sometimes called Social Politics, seeks to diagnose and deal in a practical way with current social problems. It has been accorded first place because the ordinary man becomes aware when he considers these problems in collective existence that he must reckon with a society.

"Human Ecology is concerned with man in the physical, as distinguished from the cultural or institutional, environment. The ecological order grows up as a result of competition and the coincident co-operation which inevitably arise among individuals and peoples living together in a common habitat. Ecology looks at society from the point of view of population, its growth and decline, its dispersion and settlement. From this point of view society appears primarily as a biological rather than a civic or moral order.

"Race and Culture looks at society as the ethnologist sees it, that is as an association of individuals and peoples each having a common language and possessing at the same time, as a result of intermarriage and interbreeding, certain distinguishing racial characteristics. These racial characteristics become important as human association and civilization expand since, under these conditions, they are likely to become the basis for national, class, or caste distinctions.

"Collective Behavior is concerned with the rise of new societies and new social units, in so far as they are formed in the efforts of societies and social groups to act collectively. Collective Behavior studies social movements and the tentative organizations by which they carry on before they have become fully institutionalized. Most social movements tend in the long run to terminate in institutions.

"Social Institutions has been regarded by some as the only proper subject of a sociological science. A sociology so conceived tends to be identified with social anthropology or ethnology. Ethnology seeks to study *(Consult bibliography)* institutions historically while sociology studies them comparatively.

"Socialization of the Individual relates the person to society. It shows what society does to the individual and what the person can do with society. Man is portrayed as the creature, carrier, creator, and manipulator of culture.

"It should be noted that the divisions included in this classification of subject-matter are not independent of each other, but are interdependent and overlapping."[1]

In this example of underlining, the main points are underscored. Note the question marks in the margin, indicating the reader's doubt concerning the truth or clarity of the underscored material. Note also the marginal entry opposite the sentence underscored with a double line. The reader evidently intended to consult another textbook for information about the item underlined.

In your reading you should contribute your own reactions to the subject-matter and list the follow-up work you might do. Underlining and marginal symbols will help you to accomplish these purposes. They will also help you to review any part of the textbook from time to time.

---

[1] From "Introduction" by Samuel Smith to *Principles of Sociology*, edited by Alfred McClung Lee. Published by Barnes & Noble, Inc.

CHAPTER FOUR

NOTE-TAKING

"Boiling down ideas to a few words is a practical test of your understanding of the material. You cannot say in a few words what you do not know and thoroughly understand. It is a very thoughtful type of study. ... Relationships are more clearly seen when the skeleton is divested of unimportant detail. The labor of writing is reduced if the thought is in condensed form. You should strive, therefore, in taking notes to achieve as great condensation as is consistent with clearness."—**C. C. Crawford***

Time for Taking Notes. Take notes when you read or listen to an important point you wish to remember. If you are reading and underlining a textbook that you own, write down the chief ideas you have underscored. When listening to a lecture, observe the speaker's emphasis on an idea, as disclosed by his tone of voice, deliberate pauses, and repetition of a point. Then re-state the idea in a few words. Another excellent suggestion is to read about the topic before the lecture and check your notes as soon as possible after the lecture. You may also take notes of ideas that occur to you: many students find it helpful to record such ideas immediately while writing essays or examination papers. Otherwise, they might forget their best thoughts on the subject.

Use of Notebooks. Loose-leaf notebooks are best, and the size 11″ x 8½″ is generally preferable to other

---

* From *Methods of Study* by C. C. Crawford. Used by permission of the Author.

sizes. Paste index tabs in several places, dividing the notebook into sections, and write the names of the topics or subjects on these tabs. Write plainly, so that it will be easy to read, or better still, typewrite your notes. Use main headings, and indented sub-headings; also, underline the most important items. If you have several notebooks, paste labels on the cover page and on the back of the binding. On these labels, list the subjects dealt with in the notebook. In this way, no matter whether your notebooks are lying flat or are standing on end, you will be able to select promptly the one you want.

Use of a Card System. Keep all cards arranged in order, according to subject and topic. You may either use indented sub-headings, or number the points on each card as follows: 1, 1a, 1b, etc., 2, 2a, 2b, 2c, etc. Insert special index cards, large size, or cards with gummed tabs, to separate topics from one another and to make quick reference possible. These special index cards should, of course, be filed in alphabetical order, each placed at the beginning of a new topic. As a rule, it is best to insert a new large card whenever a large unit of subject-matter is begun. None of the cards should ordinarily deal with more than one main unit of thought. Be sure to number the cards. If several cards deal with the same point, number the first one (1a), the second one (1b), the third one (1c), and so on. New cards dealing with the same item can then be numbered with the next letter of the alphabet and inserted in their proper places in the series.

Organization of Notes. Put together notes which belong together. If you use pages of a notebook, at random, for notations, you will soon be confused by the disorderly arrangement of data. Systematize note-making; keep in one section all notes concerning one topic, and all notes related to one subject. It may be that your data are useful for the study of more than one subject. If so, devise a cross reference system: in the proper place, in notebooks or in card files, insert a blank sheet or card, and indicate thereon the exact spot where you can locate additional data on the topic. In some cases, it may be advisable to make duplicate copies of notes that are useful in the study of several subjects.

Clarity and Brevity. In noting a fact, use enough words or sentences so that you can later return to the notation and immediately understand its import. Underline the significant items; write legibly in ink, or use the typewriter. Clarity and brevity are necessary for good note-making.

Language Usage. When making notes, explain ideas in your own words. Put down the significant items you read or hear in brief points, clear, complete sentences, and a simple vocabulary. Avoid unnecessary words. Abbreviate only if you feel there will never be any doubt as to what an abbreviation represents. Common abbreviations include: ref. (reference); et al. (and others); N. B. (note well); e.g. (for example); bk. (book); .·. (therefore); p. (page); etc. (and so forth); q. (question); v. (see); v. s. (see above); vs. (against); sc. (namely); sq. (the following); q. v. (which see).

Remember that the construction of too many notes destroys their value. Restrict yourself to the essentials; weigh and consider the relative importance of items; select the chief facts and ideas; avoid repetition.

Sources of Information. Write down the sources of the original material which you are summarizing in your notes. Later, you may wish to refer to these sources, and you will also know to whom items of data should be credited.

If you make notes in the margins of a textbook, to summarize the content, copy these notes in your notebook. You may then have a rough outline of the book,

in your own words, to be reviewed at a glance. Indicate
the pages from which the notes were copied.

Review of Notes. Your personal reactions to data
should be included in your notes, briefly and to the point.
From time to time, you may review such material and
compare it with your current impressions. Review many
notes at one sitting, thus unifying them in your mind.
The review and revision of notes, immediately after writing them, are especially advantageous.

CHAPTER FIVE

OUTLINING

> "Summarizing is difficult work. In its highest form it becomes a rare literary art as well as a beautiful evidence of clear thinking. The man who can seize upon the essentials of a situation, a case, a book, and report these briefly and at the same time clearly is valuable to society."—Hall-Quest*

Advantages of an Outline. Outlines may be brief resumés of a particular topic, or they may be complete summaries of entire subjects, such as comprehensive printed outlines of various subjects.[1] Compare your outline with good printed outlines. You will note at once ways to improve your work. Printed outlines make it easy to get acquainted with numerous subjects and divergent views. They can broaden and enrich your interests and educational background. You cannot study thirty, forty, or a hundred subjects in college, but you can readily obtain the essentials of them from printed outlines. You can get an idea of a subject before deciding whether or not to study it intensively. You can use printed outlines as companion books to improve your understanding of textbooks and lectures. By presenting the points of view of many authorities, a good printed outline encourages critical thinking and open-mindedness.

The Form of an Outline. A loose-leaf ring or spring notebook, with sheets 11″ x 8½″, is usually satisfactory.

---

* From *Supervised Study in the Secondary School* by A. L. Hall-Quest. Used by permission of the publishers, The Macmillan Company, New York.

1 For examples of authoritative printed summaries, see several titles in the *College Outline Series,* published by Barnes & Noble Inc., New York.

Use a systematic arrangement of items, with main headings, subheadings, and subordinate headings. The following is a suggestive form.

OUTLINE OF TOPIC .... (name of topic)
    Introductory:

        Purpose or nature of the subject-matter.
          General:
          Specific:

        Sources of the data:
          1.
          2.
          3. etc.

I. First main idea of the topic being outlined.

    A. Significant fact, opinion, or evidence supporting this idea

        1. Sources leading to A
        2. Important item relating to A

            a. Subordinate data in support of 2
            b. Additional data in support of 2

                (1) Item relating to b
                    (a) Item relating to (1)
                    (b) Second item relating to (1)
                (2) Item relating to b

    B. Another significant fact, opinion, or evidence supporting main idea I

        1. Sources leading to B
        2. Important item relating to B
        3. etc.

    C. Etc.

II. Second main idea of the topic being outlined.

    A. etc.

    B. etc.

Conclusions (or summary of chief points) :

      1.

      2.

      3.

      4. etc.

Chief references :.. ...

Note that in the above example, the items are indented according to their relative importance. If an item requires more than one line, the rest of the item is also indented so that the first word of the second line is just below the first word of the first line. All indentations should be small, but large enough to be evident at a glance.

Uniformity in Outlining. Whatever system of outlining you adopt, use it uniformly in all your studies. It will soon become habitual and will serve as a basis for straight thinking. It will give you confidence in yourself. Systematic outlining frees the mind for creative effort, helps determine when a unit of work has been satisfactorily performed, and guides the processes of logical deliberation.

The Length of Outlines. The length of an outline should depend on the purpose in mind and the nature of the subject-matter. If you anticipate the need of a thorough study of a topic, include as many relevant points as possible. All statements should be clear, brief, and easy to locate.

Arrangement of Items. It is generally best to start a new page for a new division of a subject. The use of explanatory footnotes and references at the bottom of notebook pages is recommended. After outlining all the topics in each section of an outline, you may construct a general summary of the chief conclusions for the subject as a whole. These items may be followed by a list of challenging questions or problems, for further study, and an adequate bibliography of reference material.

Determination of Subdivisions. As you read or listen to an exposition of a topic, distinguish the major from the less important ideas. Set down the significant idea first, then the points most closely related to it. You will soon have a complete list of the essential subordinate topics; then go on to the next main idea. If, for any reason, you do not have time to insert any of these subordinate concepts, continue with the main facts, but leave a space, or write very brief directions, for adding the sub-topics at the earliest opportunity. When listening to a lecture, remember that it may later be difficult to recall some of the items you failed to note down. Be sure to write a word or two, indicating the general import of the ideas omitted.

CHAPTER SIX

REVIEWING

"Of two men with the same outward experiences and the same amount of mere native tenacity, the one who thinks over his experiences most, and weaves them into systematic relations with each other, will be the one with the best memory."
—**William James***

The Necessity of Reviews. After you have thoroughly studied a subject or skill, it is generally necessary to review it at proper intervals to retain your mastery over it. Furthermore, after the lapse of time, you may return to a topic with fresh enthusiasm, new powers of interpretation, unexpected benefits. Reviewing presents an opportunity for greatly enriched learning.

Time Distribution of Reviews. Review immediately after you feel you have learned the material. Review again and again, as the practical need arises for using the subject matter you have mastered. Finally, and most important, review at frequent intervals, so that you will avoid the intellectual strain and inefficiency of cramming. Keep a record, preferably in a notebook, of the main items you have learned and those you have reviewed. You will then be able, at a glance, to decide which topics you should review once again, and how much progress you are making.

Caution. Careless reviews, permitting repetition of errors and vague prejudices, are worse than no re-

---

* From *Psychology, Briefer Course* by William James. Used by permission of the publishers, Henry Holt and Co., New York.

views at all. In reviewing, be sure you understand every idea, and relate one point to another, thus forming a unified view of the entire topic and subject. React to the materials you are reviewing, apply them to practical problems, devote more time to important points and weak spots than to subordinate units. In other words, plan your reviews carefully.

The Question-Answer Review. This way of reviewing has attractive possibilities, but requires the exercise of good judgment in the selection of the important questions to answer. Wherever possible, compare the questions you select with those in text or reference books, or in printed examinations. In this way, you will verify your choice of significant points to review. After answering a question, check the accuracy of your response. Concentrate especially on those parts (of the subject) concerning which you failed to ask questions, but which you discover to be important. Review at least once more, the points you omitted in giving answers to a question. Finally, select and review the chief questions and answers.

Emphasis on Weak Spots. It is imperative that you discover which aspects of a subject or skill you are not sure you have thoroughly mastered. Find the causes of such deficiences and resolve to prevent their recurrence. In other words, give special, critical attention to the weak spots in your process of study. Review, review, review, carefully, accurately.

Supplementary Types of Review. These include discussion, practice, writing, and teaching. Their values are obvious. Investigate the need of further study of particular items, as indicated by your capacity:

> to discuss the subject-matter intelligently,
> to meet life situations requiring mastery,
> to write about the main topics, and
> to teach others the relevant items or skills.

You may, perhaps, feel that you have learned a subject effectively, without finding it necessary to discuss, practice, or teach it with reasonable efficiency. Nevertheless, practice trying to use your learning in these ways, so that you may benefit from the excellent opportunities afforded to review the essentials.

The Use of Discrimination. It would, of course, be absurd to try to review indiscriminately all that you have learned in the past. You have probably mastered certain points so well that special review is unnecessary. Some items are less important than others; a few may be of vital import in your immediate situation. Many notations should be filed away, for reference purposes only. A great deal of what you have studied should be left for consultation in reference works.

In short, you should use discrimination in selecting the materials to review. Review periodically, those aspects of a subject:

1. Which you are not sure of, but will probably need in further study,
2. Which you know well, but feel it is important to over-learn for increased retention, and
3. Which may form the basis for new points of view, enriched appreciation, and creative work of your own.

Preliminary Tests. Test your knowledge about a topic before studying it. List the points you have previously learned about the subject; then compare the list with authoritative summaries or other reference sources. Write down some of the main questions about which you need to learn. Test yourself on these after the first few periods of study. Preliminary tests are useful before taking up a new unit of subject matter. Try to anticipate ideas before reading them.

Outline Tests. Outlining is not the best form of measurement, for it overemphasizes memorization. But outlining from memory is helpful in study. It permits the testing of the power to recall salient items of a large unit of subject-matter. Develop, from memory, outlines including main topics, evidence, sub-topics, and sources. Then use reference material as a basis for correction and revision of the outlines.

Achievement Tests. As the term implies, achievement tests relate to the measurement of the student's previous accomplishments. After completing a task, investigate the extent of your progress. Construct questions about all main points, write the answers, and check them against notes or reference works. In many subjects, standardized printed tests are available whereby you may compare your progress with that of thousands of other individuals. Underline questions you fail to answer correctly and review the relevant data repeatedly.

Many achievement tests emphasize the so-called "new-type" questions. The following examples present the most popular forms illustrated with sample questions.

Completion: The Roman god of war was named............................

Enumeration: List the members of the President's Cabinet.

Diagrammatic: Draw a diagram showing how electric power is obtained from a waterfall.

Association: The approximate number of elementary schools in the United States. ....

True-False: The Chinese armies defeated United Nations forces in December, 1950. ....

Multiple Choice: Pure water is

    (a) an element   (c) a compound

    (b) a mixture   (d) a solution

Identification: Write an M before names of musicians and an S before names of scientists.

    ....Kreisler   ....Urey

    ....Pasteur   ....Caruso

Cross Out: Cross out the numbers that do not belong in the following series:

5, 10, 20, 40, 50, 60, 80, 160, 320

Sequence: Number the following events in order of their sequence.

_____Congress of Berlin   _____Monroe Doctrine
                    _____Boxer Rebellion

Matching: Match each item in Column I with the item in Column II to which it is related. Write the correct letters in the parentheses.

(a) Thomas A. Edison   1. Military leader _____(   )
(b) Jascha Heifetz   2. Inventor _____(   )
(c) Dwight D. Eisenhower

Analogy: Knowledge is to judgment as possession is to
(1) law (2) acquisition (3) use (4) ignorance (5) dispossession

For *matching* questions, begin with the easier ones. This reduces the number of possible answers for more difficult questions. Similarly, for *completion* and *multiple-choice* problems, work on easier items may remind you of answers to remaining items.

Review through Experience. Prompt application of what you have learned to practical problems is probably the most significant form of testing. Trace the relationships between data learned and realistic personal and civic problems. Apply theories to your experience.

Use of Review Books Now Available. Comprehensive printed outlines, by eminent scholars, are available for many college subjects, including American, European, and world history, geology, economics, chemistry, physics, Shakespeare's plays, psychology, biology, English literature, journalism, education, etc.[1] A number of well-written outlines of high-school subjects are also obtainable. Change these printed outlines to meet the needs of your situation. Use them as a starting point for creative and advanced work as well as for reviews.

---

1 *College Outlines Series* published by Barnes & Noble, Inc.

CHAPTER SEVEN

WRITING

"Bad writing may be due to a bad idea, or it may be due to a failure in expression that comes from bad thinking or bad English or both. If the idea is bad, nothing can be done except burn the manuscript and discourage the writer from inflicting more wandering words upon a society already written and talked to the point of distraction."—Henry Seidel Canby*

Basic Considerations. To write well, you must think correctly, appreciate fully, understand adequately and clearly. A few suggestions are fundamental. In everything important you write, consider:

1. Purposes you have in mind,

2. Types of reader for whom you write,

3. Logical or psychological arrangement of material,

4. Elimination of unnecessary or confusing words and items; inclusion of all essentials,

5. Corrections and revisions, especially as to the choice of the best possible phrases and vocabulary, and

6. Standards of accuracy, fairmindedness, and neatness.

Types of Reports. It is often a good idea to study with the explicit purpose of writing a comprehensive

---

* From *Better Writing*, by Henry Seidel Canby. Used by permission of the publishers, Harcourt, Brace & Co., New York.

report. Reports should be concise, stressing the major problems and facts. The *book report* is a common type of report, in which you should state the title, author, objectives, arguments, main points, and essence of the volume; also selected problems, characteristics, and your own reactions. Another type of report is the *committee report,* which should state names of committee members and officers; purposes, places, and dates of meetings; contributions of individuals; points of view, procedures used in committee work; accomplishments, difficulties, and plans for the future. The *précis* is a brief summary of an argument or topic, and should include every important point. Précis paragraphs should be concise and convincing.

Essays, Articles, Theme Papers. Essays and theme papers are generally brief expositions of a topic. Introduce your subject in the first paragraph in an interesting way. Show a preference for short sentences, using, however, a variety of sentence structure. Connect each passage with the preceding sections of the material. Follow an outline, not necessarily elaborate; then, criticize and revise your work. Question the value, position, and language of each sentence, making sure that adequate space is given to important ideas, and not too much to subordinate ideas. As a rule, the middle sections should present your main arguments. Quote sources in footnotes and grant due credit to individuals or works definitely helpful to you. Offer opinions not as incontestable facts but only as tentative judgments. Try to make what you write practical or lifelike, including points you believe will interest anticipated readers, and adapting your choice of words to their ability and experience.

In revising your work, bear in mind the factors which distinguish effective writing. Is your material new, significant, specific, and practical? Is it original?

Can it be improved by additions or deletions? Are the main ideas emphasized? Is each sentence clear? Is there enough variety? Do the opening sentences stimulate attention? Are all points organized into a unified whole? As you rewrite, experiment with new approaches and new ways of expression.

Hints for Examinations. Be calm about examinations. Remember that they have constructive purposes, such as the guidance of your future study, the rectification of weak spots, and the stimulation of systematic preparation. The following suggestions should help you demonstrate the extent of your progress in a subject:

1. Read and follow all directions carefully.

2. Look through the whole test, noting the parts that seem most difficult.

3. Do the easy parts first, as well as the parts that count most, unless you are instructed to answer the questions in order.

4. Before you answer a question, read it again to make sure you know its meaning and implications.

5. Reject the temptation to guess the answer unless you have an honest basis for believing it to be probably correct.

6. Whenever you can do so quickly, associate questions with each other and with as many important ideas as you can develop.

7. Write legibly; waste no words; waste no time, but do not hurry too much.

8. Take time to go over your work, in every part of the test. You may discover omissions or errors.

In examinations which require extensive writing, you may do well to jot down a few words, on the test paper, suggesting the chief points to be considered in your answer. This procedure may help you systematize the answer, indicating a comprehensive mastery of the topic. Even in new-type tests, which require you only to check the correct answers, very brief notes of this kind may be useful to unify and clarify important items.

Research Documents. The subject you choose should be one for which you can develop genuine enthusiasm. It should be neither too easy nor too difficult. Before making a definite choice of subject, try to find out whether you will be able to obtain enough information from convenient sources to permit completion of your study within a reasonable time.

Plan your research work carefully, bearing in mind that you will have to prepare a concise, readable report, covering the following points: (1) definition of the problem; (2) your basic assumptions; (3) experiments or other activities of research conducted; (4) subjects and materials or equipment used for experiments or other research; (5) the steps or procedures used; (6) the facts and other data accumulated; (7) your conclusions; (8) the probable value of your findings.

To prepare a satisfactory research document you will have to consult many books and other sources; keep a complete record of the nature and value of each source of information; consult previous research in the same field as well as authoritative literature, to check the validity of your basic assumpions; analyze critically your procedures, data, and conclusions. In writing your report, avoid discussions that do not contribute specifically to the study, but include all essential material. The length of the report will depend on the subject investigated and the evidence needed to support your conclusions.

CHAPTER EIGHT

THE LIBRARY
and Reference Books

> "Meek young men grow up in libraries, believing it their duty to accept the views which Cicero, which Locke, which Bacon, have given; forgetful that Cicero, Locke, and Bacon were only young men in libraries when they wrote these books."
>
> **—Ralph Waldo Emerson**

Importance of the Library in Study. When we consider that at least 80% of all learning involves the use of reading materials, we sometimes wonder why more time is not devoted to studying the use of books and libraries. Students are not permitted to experiment in a chemistry laboratory without suitable preliminary instruction on the use of apparatus and materials. Yet most students have learned too little about the equipment of that most universal of all laboratories — the library. Lack of such knowledge has accounted for much inefficiency and failure in mental work.

Consequently, this chapter is devoted to a discussion and description of the library as it is found in schools, colleges, and cities of the United States. It describes the organization and arrangement of materials, the card catalog, the Decimal Classification, and certain basic reference tools essential to the learning process.

Library Organization. Although American libraries differ in size, quality, details of organization, purpose, etc., there are certain elements common to most libraries.

For example, the quarters of all libraries include reading rooms and book stacks. The book stacks may be "open shelf," that is, accessible to the public, or they may be "closed shelf," in which case the public is not permitted to go directly to the book shelves. There are found, usually: an order department, where books are selected and ordered; a cataloging department, where books are prepared for the shelves; a circulation department, where books are charged out to readers; and a reference department, where advisory and informational services are offered.

Regulations governing the use of library materials are now fairly uniform. Certain types of material may be used only within the library: periodicals, reference books, documents, valuable and rare items. Most of the remaining material is circulated, usually for a period of one or two weeks, and is subject to renewal for at least one additional period. To enforce prompt return of materials on dates due, a charging system is employed, which may include a borrower's card, a book pocket with a charging card, and a date-due slip. Failure to return a book on or before the date usually brings a fine of from two to five cents per day overdue. Books in great demand by classes of students or by groups of readers are placed on "reserve" and circulated, frequently, for short periods varying in length.

Types of Material. For convenience, library materials can be grouped into circulating and non-circulating materials. As a rule, most books may be borrowed for home use. These include fiction and the various types of books sometimes referred to as "class" books. Reserve books may be borrowed for home use under restrictions limiting the period from a few minutes before closing time to a few minutes after opening time the next morning.

The following types of material do not, as a rule, circulate:

1. *Reference books*. These books are usually shelved in the main reading or reference room. They are intended to be referred to for specific information rather than to be read through from cover to cover.

2. *Periodicals*. Neither current issues nor bound volumes of back issues circulate generally. Newspapers are in the same class.

3. *Government publications,* learned society publications, and other materials issued like periodicals. This class of publications is known as "serials."

4. *Pamphlets* kept in the vertical files.

5. *Rare* and restricted books kept in the vault.

You should locate these various types of material as soon as possible in the library which you expect to be using during the year.

Arrangement of Materials. Over 90% of all American libraries are classified by the Dewey Decimal Classification. This is a subject arrangement for material which makes possible speedy location of a library book. The system was invented by Melvil Dewey, an American librarian, in the latter part of the 19th century and was rapidly adopted not only by libraries in this country, but also by libraries abroad, by certain review periodicals, and by the International Institute of Brussels which is engaged in the compilation of a world bibliography. In effect, therefore, the Dewey Decimal Classification constitutes a sort of universal language for scholars; and mastery of its essential features will provide the student with a highly useful study tool.

The D. C. system, as the Dewey Decimal Classification is called, divides all of man's knowledge into ten classes, as follows:

000 General
100 Philosophy
200 Religion
300 Social sciences
400 Philology
500 Science
600 Useful arts
700 Fine arts
800 Literature
900 History

Each of these ten classes is divided into ten divisions, for example:

030 encyclopedias; 070 journalism — are two divisions of the 000 class
150 psychology; 170 ethics — are divisions of the 100 class
330 economics; 370 education — belong in the 300 (social science) class
420 English language is a division of the philology (400) class
510 mathematics; 540 chemistry; 570 biology — are science divisions
630 agriculture; 640 home economics — are useful arts divisions
750 painting; 780 music — are fine arts divisions
820 English literature; 840 French literature — are literature divisions
910 travel; 930 ancient history — are history divisions

Each of these hundred divisions is further subdivided into 10 sections, for example:

In the 510 (mathematics) section, 511 is arithmetic; 512 algebra, etc.
In the 780 (music) section, 781 is theory; 784 is vocal music, etc.
In the 930 (ancient history) section, 931 is China; 932 Egypt, etc.

Now each of these 1,000 sections is further subdivided into 10 sub-sections, and each of these 10,000 sub-sections is further subdivided into 10 sub-sub-sections, etc. Thus you can find a number on the back of a book which reads

512.21 ("five twelve point twenty-one")

and means

Equations, 1st to 4th degrees.

Well, what of it, you ask. Can any one be expected to go around carrying 100,000 sub-sub-sections in his head in order to find a book easily in a library? Fortunately, that isn't necessary. By means of an interesting mnemonic scheme developed by Dewey it is possible to learn the meanings of only a score of figures and with this little learning to locate books on many subjects quickly.

What figures should the average library user know who has no intention of becoming a librarian? Well, he should start with the ten classes given at the beginning of this discussion, and then memorize the following general form numbers:

01 in a number means "philosophy of"
philosophy of history is 901; philosophy of science is 501:

02 in a number means "outlines of"
202 means outline of religion; 702 outline of art:

03 in a number means "dictionary of"
thus 803 dictionary of literature:

04 in a number means "essays about"
404 essays on language:

05 in a number means "periodicals on"
905 periodicals on history:

06 in a number means "society transactions and proceedings"
506 scientific society proceedings:

07 in a number means "study of" or "teaching of"
307 study of social sciences; 807 teaching of literature:

08 in a number means "collections"
808 collections of literature:

09 in a number means "history of"
109 History of Philosophy

If you don't want to remember all nine of these, remember 03, 07, and 09.

After this there are just two sets of special form numbers. First, the so-called geographical numbers:

> England is always 2
> Germany is always 3
> France is always 4

The history of Europe is 940.

> The history of England is 942
> The history of Germany is 943
> The history of France is 944

In literature, where most of the numbers are devoted to Europe anyway, the continent number is taken for granted, and thus,

> English literature is 820
> German literature is 830
> French literature is 840

The other set of form numbers relates to literary forms:

> poetry is always 1
> drama is always 2
> fiction is always 3
> essays are always 4

Now, assuming you have memorized all the figures given, walk into your library and go directly to the shelves. Locating these miscellaneous books will be easy:

> A volume of plays by G. Bernard Shaw (822)
> Will Durant's *Story of Philosophy* (109)
> The Bible (220)
> Thomson's *Outline of Science* (502)
> Cheyney's *History of England* (942)

In many public libraries two classes of books frequently are given no numbers. Fiction is merely marked "F" and arranged alphabetically on the shelves by the authors' last names. Biography may be marked "B," or "92," or "920" but it is always arranged alphabetically, not by authors, but by the name of the person about whom the book is written.

Books are, therefore, arranged on the shelves of most libraries by the Dewey Decimal classification in numerical order, and in each number, alphabetically by author. For intelligent use of library shelves a minimum mastery of this universal scheme of library classification is urged. In addition to the numbers already mentioned, the following will be useful for reference:

310 Statistics	720 Architecture
320 Political sciences	760 Engraving
390 Customs, costume	790 Amusements
423 English dictionaries	810-19 American Literature
520 Astronomy	830 German literature
530 Physics	850 Italian literature
540 Chemistry	860 Spanish literature
550 Geology	870 Latin literature
580 Botany	891.7 Russian literature
590 Zoology	950 History of Asia
610 Medicine	960 History of Africa
620 Engineering	970 History of North America
670 Manufacturers	973-79 History of United States
690 Building	980 History of South America

Index to Materials. The index to the American library is the card catalog, often called a dictionary catalog, which is found in a special lobby or in the main reading room arranged in rows of drawers. Even to many seasoned scholars this library tool is still something of an awesome wonder. But it, like the classification scheme just described, is built on comparatively simple principles.

The first and most important of these principles is the alphabetic arrangement. With few exceptions, card catalogs are arranged so that authors, titles, subjects, and cross references are in one alphabet. The filing is generally based on alphabetic order except in the following cases:

1. Historical subjects are arranged chronologically.
2. Abbreviations are filed as if they were spelled out.

3. Articles like "the" and "a" in a title are disregarded.
4. Names beginning with "Mc" are filed as though they began with "Mac."
5. Alphabetizing is word by word rather than letter by letter, so that
   New York comes before Newark
   New Hampshire comes before Newfoundland.

There are other little rules, many of which you can not hope to remember. But the warning behind these rules is obvious: do not easily admit to yourself that a certain book is not in the library until you have carefully canvassed the card catalog.

There are at least three possible places in the card catalog where your book may be indexed. It may be found under the last name of the author, under the title of the book, or under the subject of the book. Generally speaking, the author card contains the most information about your book, and is, therefore, known as the main entry. In most libraries, cards printed by the Library of Congress in Washington are used. Here is a reproduction of an "L.C." card, and an interpretation of it:

Shores, Louis, 1904—
    Basic reference sources; an introduction to materials and methods. With a chapter on science reference sources by Helen Focke. Chicago, American Library Association, 1954.
    ix, 378 p.   25 cm.
    "Based on the author's Basic reference books".
    Includes Reading list (s)
    1. Reference books-Bibl. 2. Libraries—Reference dept.
    2. Title.
      Z1035. S49   1954   028.7   53-7487
      Library of Congress   [60]

Fɪɢ. 5. The card reproduced above has been reduced from the normal size of 3" x 5". Be sure to look at a copy of the book listed on this card. It will help you to select the best reference book for every purpose.

On the top line is the Dewey Decimal classification number and the author's full name, followed by the date of his birth. Since the date of his death is not given, this means that he is still living. The second line reproduces the title from the title page exactly. The next three items comprise the **imprint,** that is, place of publication, publisher, and date, exactly as they appear at the bottom of the title page. The line below is called the **collation,** and tells you there is a preface of nine pages numbered in Roman numerals, and that there are 398 pages of text. The size, or height, of the book is 25 centimeters.

Below this line are items of interest chiefly to librarians. Headings 1. and 2. are subjects under which you can find catalog cards for this book. In all, there are at least four cards in the catalog for this book under the following letters: **(S)**—author; **(R)**—subject; **(L)**—subject **(B)**—title. The number Z1035.S49 is the Library of Congress classification, which is usually typed in the upper left hand corner as well. By means of the Library of Congress Catalog number, 53-7487, the librarian orders this card. The remaining number is a copyright number, all books copyrighted being registered in the Library of Congress.

In addition to author, title, and subject cards, the average card catalog has "cross reference" cards. There are two kinds of cross references:

Twain, Mark

see

Clemens, Samuel Langhorne

In which the reader is referred from the name or heading under which he looked to the name or heading under which the book is entered in the card catalog.

and

School libraries, see also

Children's Literature
Libraries, Children's
Libraries and Schools

In which the reader is referred from the heading under which he found some material to other related headings under which he may find additional material.

Periodicals and Indexes. Although the card catalog frequently lists periodicals in the library, it almost never indexes the contents of these periodicals. For this purpose there exist "cumulative" indexes issued in periodical and book form. The most frequently used and therefore the most useful periodical index is the *Readers' Guide* published semi-monthly and cumulated frequently into monthly, bi-monthly, semi-annual, annual, and biennial volumes. It is an index to over 100 American and Canadian periodicals most frequently found in American libraries and in American homes. Among the magazines indexed are the *American, Atlantic Monthly, National Geographic, Time, Saturday Evening Post,* etc. All articles are indexed under subject and author (in some cases under title) and in one alphabet much as in the card catalog. It is, therefore, possible to locate a current article by Philip Wylie in the **Reader's Guide** by looking under "W." It is also possible to find several articles on the Tennessee Valley Authority by looking under "T." Important is an understanding of the short form of reference used in these indexes: Sci Am 149:843-5 Ag '33 means **Scientific American**, volume 149, pages 843 through 845 in the August, 1933, issue.

Another more specialized periodical index is the *International Index*. In spite of the fact that the covers of this index are colored tan and those of the *Readers' Guide* are colored green, even advanced students make no distinction between the two. Whereas the latter indexes 100 American and Canadian popular magazines, the *International* indexes over 250 American and foreign scholarly magazines, largely in the fields of language, literature, and history. Otherwise, the arrangement is the same in both indexes, except that the *International* appears only bi-monthly.

There are special periodical indexes for various fields. Examples of indexes to the periodicals of special subjects are:

> *Education Index*
>
> *Art Index*
>
> *Applied Science and Technology Index*
>
> *Public Affairs Information Service* (P. A. I. S.) (Social Sciences)
>
> *Agricultural Index*

Two indexes of special interest because they differ in form are the *New York Times Index*, and the *Book Review Digest*. The first of these is really an index to all news of the *Times*. In this index, a citation II 1:7 means section two of the Sunday issue, page one, column 7. The *Book Review Digest* is more than an index to book review periodicals. Under each current book a digest of the book is given in a paragraph, which is followed by excerpts from leading reviews. Following each excerpt, a figure indicating the total length of the review in number of words is indicated, and, what is more interesting, a plus for favorable or a minus for unfavorable reviews is added.

General Reference Books. The two most frequently consulted unabridged dictionaries are the *Merriam-Webster New International* and *Funk and Wagnalls New Standard*. Although they look alike in size and general format, they differ in many respects. Webster's was first issued fully a half century before its rival. If you compare the two dictionaries you will note these significant differences among others.

The most scholarly dictionary of the English language is the famous *Oxford English Dictionary* which was seventy years in the making. Its special feature is word history illustrated by nearly two million quotations from the great literature of the English people.

A good encyclopedia, properly used, is the best starting source for all study. It includes a systematic summary of all knowledge significant to mankind. Its articles are usually written by the leading authorities on each subject. Its bibliographies introduce you to the best literature in each field. A smart orientation for a new course is to read a good encyclopedia's article on the subject before you go to the first class.

Most encyclopedias are arranged alphabetically by subject. But many more subjects are treated in an encyclopedia than there are separate articles. Failure to recall this one fact often prevents efficient use of this basic reference tool. For example, **Encyclopedia Britannica** has 40,000 separate articles in volumes 1-23. But **Britannica** provides information on no fewer than 500,000 subjects. (There are continuous plate revisions with frequent reprintings to keep the work up-to-date.) Therefore, if you are looking up information on a comparatively small topic like **phalanx,** your chances of finding that subject in the separate articles of the first 23 volumes of the **Britannica** are no better than 2 in 25. You should immdiately consult the great index in volume 24, which also contains all of the maps in one place.

Another great set is the **Encyclopedia Americana** in 30 volumes (with continuous plate revisions). Its index is in the 30th volume, but its maps are scattered throughout the set so as to be near their related articles. Among special features the **Americana** has century articles summarizing the history of each one hundred years, under the century, e.g., **Thirteenth Century.**

A third great set is **Collier's Encyclopedia** in 20 volumes. Its last volume contains not only the index but a remarkable bibliography arranged and graded by subject bibliographers so as to enable you to progress from the point where the encyclopedia article leaves off. Other features of this set are the many illustrations, both in black and white and color, placed on the same pages as the related text, and the attention to modern scientific and technological subjects.

There are several other good encyclopedia sets, and nearly all of them issue yearbooks to supplement the information in the main work. An example of this type of yearbook is the **Britannica Book of the Year.** There are also handy one-volume encyclopedias like the **Columbia Encyclopedia** which is alphabetically arranged, and the **Lincoln Library of Essential Information,** which is classified in arrangement, with an alphabetical index in back.

Other Reference Books. It will pay you to spend an hour exploring the books on the open shelves of a reference room. In this collection alone is the answer to nearly every question that comes up in connection with study and investigation.

Consider the almanac, for example, with its miscellany of facts and figures on government, business, education, art, sports, and almost any subject. Two leading examples are the **World Almanac,** with index in front; and the **Information Please Almanac,** with index in back. To supplement these two for statistics, use the U. S. Government's **Statistical Abstract** for this country and the **Statesman's Yearbook,** for other countries.

Gazetteers are geographical dictionaries and two leading examples are the **Columbia-Lippincott Gazetteer** and the **Webster Geographical Dictionary**. Guide books are intended to aid the traveller with locating sights, accommodations, and good food. A famous name among guide books is **Baedeker,** and there is a Baedeker book for nearly every place abroad. For the United States, **Guide to America,** issued by the American Automobile Association, is compact. The third and probably most important type of geographical reference book is the atlas.

To use an atlas properly it is necessary to know whether the index is all together in one place or whether each map has its own index. It is also important to understand the difference between a Mercator projection (in which Greenland appears to be larger than the United States) and an equidistant map. Some good atlases are Goode's **World Atlas**; Rand McNally **Cosmopolitan World Atlas**; Hammond **Ambassador World Atlas**. Shepherd's **Historical Atlas** features maps that describe the world at key periods from 1450 B.C., and Muir's **Historical Atlas** performs a comparable service from the middle ages to the present.

Notables still living can be found in the British **Who's Who,** which is published annually, or in **Who's Who in America,** published biennially, depending upon their nationality. Notables who are dead can be found in the **Dictionary of National Biography,** if they are British, or in the **Dictionary of American Biography.** If you aren't certain whether or not a notable is still alive and don't know his nationality it is better to go to what is called a universal biographical source. A good example is **Webster's Biographical Dictionary.**

About 7,000 standard reference titles exist. No one can hope to know them all very well. The ones described should enable you to answer ninety per cent of your questions. For the remaining ten per cent consult **Basic Reference Sources,** the book described on the catalog card discussed earlier in the chapter (page 45).

CHAPTER NINE

Study of
ENGLISH

> "In the long run the secret of study resides in our ability to bathe our thought, our task, our lesson in the stream of interest. The way to study successfully and joyously is to be interested in the thing that claims our attention."—F. C. Lockwood*

ENGLISH COMPOSITION

The Importance of Practice. It is said that some persons have a natural gift for writing, and that others are naturally handicapped in this field. Yet, many of the most skillful writers have had to work laboriously before they could develop the proper style and content. Regardless of the extent of one's natural gifts, the safest and best way to insure efficiency in composition is to study and practice.

Careful Choice of Topics To Write About. There must be a great number of diversified topics in which you are interested. But at the moment, perhaps you cannot think of one special topic about which to write. If so, use a logical system of reference. Think about——

A. *Personal Affairs*: what you saw or heard; what happened to you; successes you enjoyed; ambitions you developed; disappointments you encountered; problems of a personal nature; interesting trips; conversations; people you met; emotions, fears,

---

* From *The Freshman and His College* by F. C. Lockwood. Used by permission of the publishers, D. C. Heath and Co., New York.

beliefs, attitudes; and so on. Surely in thinking about these types of experience, you will find many topics to write about.

B. *Impersonal Interests*: events and problems in the fields of government, art, music, science, philosophy, literature, recreation, business, economics, education, recent history, and so on.

List a number of topics in which you might be interested. Jot down two or three ideas about each of them. Choose a topic about which you feel you have something really substantial to say. You are now ready to begin the preliminary work of composition.

If you have a topic assigned to you, associate it with some of the factors under A or B.

Systematic Organization of Ideas. The proper organization of your thoughts is a necessary foundation of your composition. Practice organizing your ideas in a variety of ways, always bearing in mind the following questions:

1. How can I begin so as to stimulate the reader's interest?

2. What are the most important points to develop in the body of the composition? How can interest be sustained?

3. In what order should these points be presented?

4. How much space should I give one item as compared with other items?

5. What would be the best way to bring the composition to a close?

Outlines are excellent helps in organizing your thoughts. When you begin to write an essay, you should almost invariably construct a number of different outlines so that you can choose the best. Be sure to think about the preceding five questions whenever you make an outline. Of course, you need not follow a systematic outline rigidly; vary from it if you find the style or content will be improved thereby.

Adaptation of Material to Many Types of Readers. It is good policy to practice with topics that may be of interest to several types of readers. For example, the topic of proper family relationships is of interest to children as well as to adults. Why not write two essays on such a subject, one addressed to children, the other to parents? Another good experiment is to read an editorial in your daily paper, noting points with which you agree and those with which you disagree. Then re-write the editorial, using your own words, and bearing in mind the different kinds of readers who may read the paper. Try to make your article more convincing, expressive, and practical than the original, and more appealing to the types of readers involved.

Evaluation through Comparison with Work of Others. Some of the best writers have learned most through repeated comparisons between their work and the work of other authors. Here are two kinds of exercise suggestive of the best way to practice such comparison:

1. Using only two or three words, jot down the main idea in each sentence of a well-written composition. Choose a long composition for this exercise so that you will not remember too many of the author's words. Without looking at the original, rewrite the ideas in your own words. Use the best words you can find. Consult the dictionary and the thesaurus. After you have finished re-writing the whole composition, compare your results with the original. Note especially the differences

in organization of content, choice of words and sentences, and sentence structure. Finally, re-write your own material to improve its effectiveness and style. This time, you may use some of the words of the original, but not the phrases unless you enclose them in quotation marks. Try to equal or excel the skill of the author.

2. Analyze a well-written essay, and list its special merits. Consider:

    a. choice of words,

    b. variations in structure of sentences and paragraphs,

    c. flow of ideas, and how it is obtained,

    d. phrases that make a paragraph highly effective,

    e. ways in which the author holds the reader's interest, and

    f. other factors that make the essay exceptionally expressive or convincing. Are the materials and style practical, concise, realistic, filled with variety, logically persuasive?

Now put the essay aside. Re-write the ideas, without notes, in your own words. Compare each paragraph with the original. Note differences in organization, structure of sentences, word selection, connecting links between paragraphs, etc. Re-write, and compare again with the original.

The Development of Spontaneity. Spontaneity is one of the vital factors in writing. Practice writing about all sorts of topics that come to mind. When you get an idea, write one or two paragraphs about it. When you meet interesting people or have unusual experiences, write about them. At first, you will probably want to revise everything you write, correcting over and over.

Soon, however, the best work you have done should become more nearly habitual. As you write, think of the best possible words, and recall the kinds of revision you found successful in previous attempts.

Free, quick expression and effective style are generally the results of patient, attentive practice. *Remember, however, that practice makes perfect only if it is careful, critical practice.* Write frequently, until you can write with greater ease, avoiding meanwhile as many defects as you can. Read aloud what you write, and try to make it natural, eliminating flowery language or a stiff, pedantic presentation.

You should follow an outline, though not slavishly. The most effective writer is he who writes freely, relating one part to another in a unified artistic whole, reworking phrases or entire paragraphs to secure the best effects.

Standards of Writing Style and Technique. Although you should write spontaneously, you must still follow certain necessary standards of style and technique, especially the following:

1. The style should be your own, never an artificial imitation of someone else's way of writing. Write so that your friends will say, "That's just the way I should have expected you to express it." Natural style is a matter of using words with just the right emphasis and phrases with exactly the type of logic, thinking, feeling, and swing or rhythm characteristic of your manner of self-expression.

2. There ought to be only one major story or central motif in a composition. Every paragraph should bear a definite relation to the main idea; and every sentence should be connected with the chief points of the paragraph. In this way, the whole composition, and each of its parts, will be unified by a number of

inter-related ideas, well arranged, progressing from introductory to expository and closing sections.

3. Try to express every point just a little more effectively than the terms in which it first occurred to you. Think about what you are going to write: experiment in your mind, with various words, phrases, and sentences, until you can set down a natural, forceful paragraph.

4. After completion of the first draft of a composition, select the parts you believe to be the weakest. Concentrate on the improvement of these parts. Then, review the whole composition. Put it aside, and let some time elapse before you revise it again.

5. Use a variety of sentences, some brief, others longer. Too many short sentences produce an abrupt stiff style; too many long ones give the effect of monotony and artificiality. Adjust the length of the sentences to the ideas you wish to express. When two or three brief sentences together with one or two long ones seem to give the proper results, use them. A long sentence may be excellent, if it is well constructed with phrases that contribute to its force and unity.

6. Choose words carefully, considering many before deciding which are more effective. Avoid exaggeration, and try to use phrases that present your ideas in a simple, direct, smooth-flowing fashion. Reject expressions that have been overworked. Do your best to secure the effect of freshness and naturalness.

Standards of Grammar and Usage. You should, of course, keep on hand a manual of language usage, a dictionary, and a thesaurus. Consult a reference source whenever you are in doubt about punctuation, diction, sentence structure, and the use of particular words. (The chief points to remember about punctuation are presented on pp. 64-72.)

In writing, be sure that you use the correct sequence of tenses in sentences. Make your subject and verb agree. Use parallel construction for parallel ideas. Avoid split infinitives, indefinite references, and incorrect shifts in your point of view. As for punctuation, your main effort should be to improve the flow of the composition, contribute to its rhythm, and make it easier to read, more forceful and impressive. Frequent inspection of the punctuation used by the best authors will help.

Oral Expression. In conversation and public speaking, agree with others so far as you sincerely can. Avoid the chronic debater. Organize your thoughts, express them modestly but earnestly, defend them tactfully and reasonably. Avoid the effect of authority, pomposity, or declamation. Speak slowly, distinctly, but with sufficient rhythm and emphasis. Put ideas in a nutshell, a key sentence, followed or preceded by brief illustrations or related ideas. Practice speaking before different types of imaginary audiences. Be natural in tone of voice and in gestures. Avoid humor unless it is apt, to the point, appropriate to the occasion, a reinforcement of the point or argument you are making. Show respect for the intelligence of your audience, no matter who they may be. Tell your message briefly and conclude.

ENGLISH LITERATURE

Literature and Reality. Literature is worth while in so far as it reflects life. We are all interested in living realities; we enjoy skillfully-arranged language that makes characters, ideas, messages, and plots lifelike. A good story is not necessarily true, although most of the events of fiction have remarkable parallels in real life. But a good story seems true while we are reading it, unless we stop to consider that we are, after all, reading only a story. Literature is a high art when it embodies many of the qualities of life so skillfully that even the fantastic seems real.

Careful Reading. Intensive reading and critical reflection are secrets of the appreciation of literature. *After you have read prose or poetry, question yourself as to the essence of what you have read.* What was the mood of the work? Was the work pessimistic, optimistic, conservative, practical, filled with many moods? Whom would you describe as the most interesting characters? The most real? Compare people you have known with those about whom you have read. Study the ideas of the author and of his characters. Consider the motives of individuals, their methods of self-expression, the merits of their points of view.

Literary Style. You may gain enriched appreciation of an author's work if you pause to consider his most expressive phrases, his choice of words, and the flow of his composition. In time, as you try to analyze the styles of the authors whose works you read, you will learn to recognize their writings through their characteristic techniques. Select and memorize some of their best passages, the ones most appealing to you.

In analyzing style, note the most effective passages, those with more emotional strength, courage, humor, depth of thought, sorrow, fear, desperation, and other moods, those with greater feeling, poetic qualities, and suggestiveness. Compare several works of the same author. Compare the work of one author with that of others. Read aloud and, in some instances, memorize choice passages.

Analysis of the style and literary qualities of literature should not be carried to an extreme. *But discrimination among particular phrases, sections, characters, and ideas is an important integral part of true appreciation.* To appreciate fully a brilliant selection from Shakespeare, for example, you should grasp the intensity of emotion, unity of organization, aptness of phrase, and diversity of moods —all the vast differences between such literature and commonplace writing. Do not read to analyze; analyze and compare, so that you will the better enjoy and understand what you read.

Choice of Books To Read. If you are studying the history of literature, be sure to read extensively the original works of each period. It is not enough to learn about the lives and views of authors, nor even about the content of their writings. You must *read* their novels, poems, short stories, essays, speeches, and plays. Only in this way can you really master the history of literature. *Read quickly; then, re-read more slowly and carefully the most interesting and impressive works.*

To keep abreast of the best modern literature, consult book reviews, newspaper criticism, library lists of new books, reports of book clubs, and literary journals. Do considerable browsing in the library. Perhaps you will find that many appealing books have been underestimated by critics, whereas others have been greatly over-rated. *Use your own judgment, applying the highest standards to your selections.* Remember that the best seller of today may be the forgotten book of tomorrow. Read especially the authors and types of literature you believe may have lasting value, the compositions that influence most your ideas, emotions, and sense of keen appreciation.

Imagination and Appreciation. Some readers lessen their enjoyment of literature by refusing to follow where the author leads. They resist the current of a book, with constant challenge of its probability as a true account of life. They keep reminding themselves that they are reading about imaginary characters.

When you read fiction or poetry forget everything but the material itself. You will be conscious enough that it is not reality. A description of a battle is not the battle itself. But imagine the events about which you read, just as if you were a witness to them in real life. *Give your imagination and emotions free reign.* When you see a beautiful painting, you do not need to consider whether it is representative of an existing scene. You note the art and skill of the painting, its dominant character and meanings, relationships that are the product of a sensitive hand and mind. In reading a literary passage, attend likewise to its beauty, action, ideas, language, and relationships. Think with the thoughts presented by the author, feel with his characters.

A great author once said that the characters he created in his books were to him much more real than the people with whom he associated. To get the most out of literature, you must live with it and in it, without artificial reservations, skeptical abstractions, or self-limitations.

Reaction to Literature. Write reviews or resumés of the books you read. Study the author's style. Set forth your ideas about his characters, plot, language, and point of view. Write as if you were a newspaper critic, reviewing the book for your readers. Compare your criticisms with those of other critics.

Discuss the books you have read. Tell your friends about the qualities and content of works in which they might be interested. Ask them questions about the literature they have read.

A *book report* deals with a given piece of literature, more in detail than a book review does. When you study an important book, write a summary of its content, together with your reactions to each major point. In time, you will have a series of extensive book reports, to which you can later refer. Reading a good report you have written about a book is the next best thing to re-reading the book itself.

Social and Personal Background of Literature. If you know the social environment and personal background of an author, you may better understand the significance of his work. If you have read the history of the Puritans, you will be able to appreciate how the literature of their period fits into the character of the people and the conditions of their time. A study of current history will help you "spot" the propaganda as well as the beauties of contemporary works. Read periodicals and books that will provide opportunities to study many sides of controversial points of view.

Value of Keeping a Record. A literary diary is an excellent device which can help you to keep track of your changing tastes and standards. Note the dates when you read the book, the name of the author, publisher, etc., and a brief reaction to the volume as a whole. This procedure is a good check on the extensiveness as well as the quality of your readings.

JOURNALISM

The Field of Journalism. Journalism deals with the daily and weekly newspapers; periodicals; trade journals; newsmagazines and magazine digests. The suggestions pertaining to English composition may apply to the study of journalism. We may, however, consider a few special hints.

Analyses of Current Events. Study the press descriptions of local and national, as well as international, events. Re-write these descriptions in your own words, preferably in a notebook. If you review your notes, from time to time, you will broaden your background for the study of journalistic methods and processes.

Development of Writing Skills. *Try to acquire the ability to write quickly, but in an effective, organized fashion, about every question, problem, or experience that could possibly be interesting to others.* With constant practice, you should soon be able to write almost as readily as you speak.

Value of Professional Contacts. Make friends among reporters, editors, and other journalistic workers. Listen to everything they have to tell you about their methods, problems, and experiences. Visit them at home; visit their places of business. In other words, follow up as many professional contacts as you can.

Value of a Broad Background. Remember that journalists benefit from a study of stenography, government, art, economics, history, philosophy, literature, science, business management, business law, marketing, composition, public speaking, mathematics, and modern foreign languages. Any of these subjects will be an important asset to you.

CHAPTER TEN

Minimum Essentials of
PUNCTUATION

> "No man can write really well who does not punctuate well; who cannot vitally mean every punctuation mark as clearly and as vigorously as he means any word."
>
> —Arlo Bates*

The easiest way to learn how to punctuate your writing effectively is to forget about rules and concentrate on meaning. *A mark of punctuation is a conventional symbol with a definite meaning, just as a written word is a symbol with a definite meaning.* Effective punctuation is essential to good writing because it gives the reader certain meanings which are not explicitly stated by the word-symbols. You may write either "He died?" or "He died." but only your choice of period or question mark will tell the reader precisely what your words mean.

Since each mark has one meaning and only one, effective punctuation is relatively easy to master. Understand the meaning of each mark, fix it firmly in your mind, and then write exactly what you mean.

In the following summary, each mark is defined and its correct usage is illustrated by examples.[1]

BEGINNING AND END PUNCTUATION

In written English, some device is necessary to show readers where one sentence ends and another begins. To

---

* From *Talks on Writing English* by Arlo Bates. Used by permission of the publishers, Houghton Mifflin Company, Boston.
[1] For a full discussion, consult *Punctuation: A Practical Method Based on Meaning* by Robert Brittain (in *College Outline Series*) published by Barnes and Noble, Inc., 1950.

avoid having sentences run together in a meaningless jumble, we use four familiar punctuation marks.

Capital Letter. This familiar symbol means simply, "This point marks the beginning of a new sentence." Do not confuse it with the nonpunctuational capital letter used in spelling proper names or with the capital often found at the beginning of a line of verse. These do not affect meaning, and are therefore not marks of punctuation.

The Period. The period means, "This is the end of a complete statement." Do not confuse it with the *abbreviation point,* a device of spelling which shows that a particular group of letters is not a completed word-symbol but only a shortened form of the word.

Examples: Mr., Y.M.C.A., Conn.

Also, do not confuse with the *decimal point,* a spelling device used when we write a decimal fraction in Arabic figures.

Examples: 2.57   .008

The Question Mark. This mark means that the completed sentence is cast in the form of a question.

Example: Where are the snows of yesteryear?

The Exclamation Point. This mark means that the foregoing sentence is expressed with great forcefulness. If speaking, you would *exclaim* it emphatically. Use this mark with moderation; overuse indicates hysteria.

Example: Keep back from the fire!

Sentence Fragments. When a fragmentary or incomplete statement (word, phrase, dependent clause) makes complete sense by itself, treat it like a sentence, using appropriate beginning and end punctuation.

Examples: As you were.   Help!   So what?

THE FIVE PRINCIPAL INTERIOR MARKS

Inside the sentence, many situations arise in which the meaning is not made completely clear by the words alone, and to communicate our meaning exactly we use a variety of marks. The five most common ones account for the great bulk of punctuation in ordinary writing. Master these thoroughly. Note carefully that three of them contain the comma symbol, either alone or in combination, but that each is a separate and distinct mark with its own meaning.

The Single Comma. The single comma occurs with comparative rarity. It means, "At this point a small element has been omitted from the sentence," and the omitted element is always one the reader can easily supply for himself.

Examples: (a) To err is human; to forgive, divine. (b) The house was large, handsome, imposing.

In the second example, each single comma indicates the omission of the conjunction "and." In a series like this, when the final conjunction is inserted for smoother reading, it is generally better to insert the extra single comma also. (*Example:* The house was large, handsome, and imposing.) Some editors omit the final comma, but when any element in the series is a compound it is vitally necessary; therefore it seems best always to use it. (*Example:* He had red, blue and yellow, green, and gold balloons.)

Do not confuse the punctuational single comma with the comma-like symbol used in writing large numbers with Arabic figures (e.g., 125,793).

The Pair of Commas. Used more frequently than any other mark of interior punctuation, the pair of commas is perhaps the most important punctuational symbol. It means, "The element enclosed within this mark of punctuation is not essential to the grammatical structure of the sentence, and it is placed in such a position that it changes the normal order."

The *normal order* of an English sentence is: subject with its essential modifiers, verb with its essential modifiers, and object or verb·complement with its essential modifiers. When you interrupt or change this normal order by inserting a nonessential element, you must use commas to warn the reader. Because of the structure of our language, interruptive, nonessential elements occur in a wide variety of syntactical situations. The following are the principal ones.

1. Nonrestrictive clauses require the pair of commas.

Examples: (a) John, who never stopped to think before he acted, ran off immediately towards the firehouse. (The dependent clause breaks the normal order by separating verb from subject. Although it modifies the subject, it is not an essential modifier; the sentence is perfectly clear without it.) (b) He looked upon Mr. Robbin, who had less money than he, with ill-concealed contempt.

But note that restrictive clauses are not set off.

Examples: (a) One who never stops to think before he acts is apt to do some foolish things. (The dependent clause stands between subject and verb, but since it is an essential modifier of the subject, there is no violation of the normal order.) (b) He despised everybody who had less money than he.

2. Words in apposition are always interruptive, nonessential elements.

Examples: (a) Dr. John Doe, President of Blank College, was the first speaker. (b) She asked Judge Robinson, the delegate from the Civil Liberties Council, to make his report.

3. Transitional words and phrases have no grammatical function; they are merely bridges from one idea to another. Therefore, they have no normal position in the sentence and always separate two elements which belong together.

Examples: (a) This book, for example, gives a good summary of the matter. (b) The girl in the blue dress, as you say, dances well.

4. Words of direct address are nonessential and always interrupt the normal order.

Examples: (a) This point, ladies and gentlemen, is very important. (b) Come here, John, and give me a hand with this box.

5. The name of a geographical area immediately following the name of some locality within that area, and the name of a year immediately following a date within that year — these are conventionally regarded as grammatically nonessential elements which interrupt the normal order.

Examples: (a) He lived at 301 Down Street, Boston 16, Massachusetts, for many years. (b) She was born on January 27, 1938, at four o'clock in the morning.

6. A direct quotation is regarded as a nonessential, interruptive element, although this usage seems purely a convention.

Example: Johnny was shouting, "Last one in is a rotten egg," as he dived into the pool.

Note very carefully that when the nonessential, interuptive element comes either at the beginning or at the end of a sentence, *only one part of the pair of commas is visible.* The other is absorbed by the stronger initial or terminal mark.

Examples: (a) As a matter of fact, this pie is not very good. (b) I have eaten better pies, as a matter of fact.

Such nonessential elements change the normal order because normally the first thing in the sentence should be the subject with its essential modifiers, and the last thing should be the object or verb complement with its essential modifiers.

Examples: (a) When she had finished with her chores, Mary went to bed. (b) Mary went to bed when she had finished her chores. (There are no commas in the second example because the modifying clause is exactly where it belongs.)

The Comma Plus Coördinating Conjunction. This mark is normally used in only one situation: that is, in the middle of a compound sentence. It means, "At this point one independent clause has been completely stated, and the second is about to begin."

Examples: (a) John has gone to the movies, but Herbert is at home. (b) Let us not be too hasty in our judgments, for there is more to this than meets the eye.

The Semicolon. This mark has exactly the same meaning as the comma plus coördinating conjunction. Either may be used to show the mid-point of a compound sentence; the difference is purely rhetorical.

Examples: (a) John has gone to the movies; Herbert is at home. (b) Let us not be too hasty in our judgments; there is more to this than meets the eye.

There are two important variations.

1. To clarify the meaning of a complicated sentence, one may sometimes arbitrarily raise the comma plus conjunction to a semicolon plus conjunction.

Example: The musicians began to beat upon a weird collection of instruments, including a drum made of elephant hide, a hollowed log, and a kind of tambourine; and a beautiful dark-skinned girl, after the noise had been going on for several minutes, rose swiftly and began to dance.

2. When the elements in a series are long and complicated, one may sometimes arbitrarily raise the single comma (which shows the omission of a conjunction between elements in the series) to a semicolon.

Example: He was proud of the fact that he had written one book about India, filled with elaborate descriptions of scenery, architecture, and unusual customs; a longer book describing a journey through South America, in the course of which he was lost for nine days in the Andes; and a whole series of travel articles for various magazines.

The Colon. The colon means, "The words which follow will give a fuller explanation of what has just been said."

(a) Johnny behaved very badly: he shrieked, made hideous faces, and threw his pudding on the floor. (b) Mrs. James found herself in a quandary: she could neither pay for the unwanted goods nor return them to the shop. (c) Please remember to bring me four articles: a comb, a razor, a toothbrush, and a cake of soap.

It is customary to place a colon after the salutation at the beginning of a formal letter or speech. This has nothing to do with punctuation; it is merely a formal convention.

Examples: Dear Sir: Mr. Chairman, Ladies, and Gentlemen:

OTHER MARKS OF PUNCTUATION

The Single Dash. This is exactly the reverse of the colon in meaning. It means, "The preceding elements in this sentence explain more fully the statement now to be made."

Examples: (a) She could neither pay for the unwanted goods nor return them to the shop—she was indeed in a quandary. (b) A comb, a razor, a toothbrush, and a cake of soap—these are the four articles I want you to bring.

Parentheses. When used to enclose any element in a sentence, this mark means, "The normal order of the sentence is here changed by the insertion of a nonessential element so phrased that it shows little, if any, grammatical relationship to the rest of the sentence." This is a much stronger mark than the pair of commas.

Example: The entire city (population 47,000 in 1951) was placed under martial law.

Pair of Dashes. This extremely emphatic mark means, "The normal order is here interrupted with great violence, either syntactical or emotional."

Example: The growing pressure of population—London rose from around 100,000 at the beginning of Elizabeth's reign to double that number under her successor—had long since pushed the inhabitants outside the circle of the walls.

Note carefully that sometimes only the first half of the pair of dashes is visible. This is the case when a sentence is violently broken and never completed.

Examples: "Help!" she screamed. "He is——" The roar of the siren drowned her voice.

Quotation Marks. These marks mean, "The enclosed element comprises the exact words of some person whom the author is quoting." Single quotation marks enclose a quotation within a quotation.

Examples: (a) "Julius Caesar," continued the speaker, "was always ready to boast, 'I came, I saw, I conquered'." (b) The German expression is "butterfly weeks," a delightfully giddy term, far more delicate and witty in its connotations than our sentimental "honeymoon." (Note that this writer is quoting the exact words of a whole group of people. This use of quotation marks applies also to slang when used in formal writing.)

The Brackets. The element enclosed within a pair of brackets is an explanatory remark inserted into a quotation by the quoter.

Examples: "Handel," says Dr. Brown, "was the only English composer [Handel was English only by adoption] who can be ranked with the supreme masters."

If you ever need to use parentheses within parentheses, you should arbitrarily change the inner pair of parentheses into brackets to avoid confusion.

Three Dots. This mark means, "At this point, certain elements are purposely omitted from the quotation, but without any suggestion of violence."

Example: (a) "Well, it is hard, but I..." His voice trailed away into an inaudible whisper. (b) "Love the Lord thy God... [and] thy neighbor."

SOME NONPUNCTUATIONAL DEVICES

The Hyphen. This is a spelling symbol used to join two or more words into one compound word, or at the end of a line when a word is broken into syllables.

Examples: (a) a three-year-old child (b) forty-seven

The Apostrophe. This is a spelling symbol used in writing contractions, possessives, and some plurals; it generally indicates the omission of one or more letters.

Examples: (a) can't (b) the boy's hat (c) the boys' hats (d) five X's

Remember also the following nonpunctuational devices mentioned earlier: the abbreviation point, the decimal point, the comma-like symbol used in writing large numbers, and the capital letter used in spelling proper names or at the beginning of a line of verse.

CHAPTER ELEVEN

Study of
THE FINE ARTS

> "Stated simply, every artist tries to convey what he is feeling. Inspired by the thing that is moving him, he invents ways and means of expressing it, often at the cost of long-continued and herculean efforts. Thus, technique is not a fixed thing with unchangeable rules, but a new invention for each work of art with rules of its own that extend no further than that work."
>
> —**Alexandre Devignes***

Nature of the Fine Arts. The fine arts include architecture, music, painting, poetry, sculpture, drama, and dancing. The fine arts are kinds of activity which express our creative impulses and appeal to our sense of beauty or pleasurable appreciation. Fine arts deal with the ideal, the imagined, the free efforts of the artist to achieve the aesthetic effects he desires. The artist takes pleasure in producing; the witness or consumer of art takes pleasure in observing. These pleasures are quite apart from the practical utility of artistic work. The professional musician is an artist not because he earns money by means of his art, but because he gives beauty to others and can himself appreciate the beauty he produces.

Spontaneity. *Spontaneity is an essential element of all the fine arts.* Even professional artists cannot succeed simply by mastering set rules or techniques. You must

---

* From *Ishtar of the Seven Gates* by Alexandre Devignes. Used by permission of the publisher.

73

form the habit of expressing yourself as best you can. Draw spontaneously. In music, stress rhythmic movement. Remember that the important method of the artist is that of doing things on impulse, stating his own meaning in terms of the particular medium of the art. Put all your thought and energy, all your attention and interest, wholeheartedly in the art you are studying.

Progress from Simple to Complex. You will waste time and become discouraged if you attempt tasks that are far too difficult for you to accomplish. In music, for instance, begin with the melodies you can readily understand; then, you may proceed to study those just a little more difficult. So, too, in painting or sculpture, it is best to begin with the simpler familiar objects. Even if you are not studying to become an artist, but only to get acquainted with and enjoy the fine arts, begin with the works you can easily master. *Above all else, never become discouraged.* Others have learned the most difficult or intricate aspects of an art; you can learn them, too. By arranging your efforts in a scale of gradually increasing difficulty, the tasks that now seem insuperably beyond your ability, will become relatively simple to perform. Patience and hard work are the chief requirements.

Emphasis on Meanings and Effects. Every art has rules and techniques. It would, however, be a great mistake to assume that the important part is the technical aspect. On the contrary, the important part is the message of an artistic work, its meaning, its total result, its effect as a whole on the consumer of art. It is, of course, necessary to master certain techniques in music or in graphic art, or in sculpture. But these techniques should be used for only one purpose: *to improve the meaning of the work as a whole.* Technique is a means to an end, not an end in itself.

Instead of stressing rules, methods, and techniques, important as these may sometimes be, emphasize the composite general message of your work of art. If you are drawing or studying a portrait, devote your attention mainly to the larger general effect, the meaning as a whole, the message. Later, you can inspect outstanding lines, colors, and rhythms. Still later, you can attend to the harmonization of each detail contributing to the beauty of the production.

Vary your methods of work. *Never be satisfied until you secure precisely the effects, the final pleasing results, you want.* Follow the example of the genius, who possesses infinite patience, not resting until every minute point gives him the exact meanings and outcomes he is eager to achieve.

Expression of Experience. In learning an art, be sure to be sincere in your performance. Just as you write or express opinions that are truly yours, so express your real emotions, thoughts, and character through your art work. Avoid insincerity, artificiality, and "copycat" efforts. If you have no message to deliver, or if you feel disinclined to express yourself, wait until a more opportune occasion arises. On the other hand, it may be possible to get yourself into the mood for creative work. *Make sure, however, that it is an expression of your experience, your feelings, your personality.*

Rhythm and Coördination. Both in appreciation and in production of art, rhythm and coördination are important. Concentrate on these two aspects of the art you are studying. In music, phrase rhythm and rhythmic movement (particularly, body-movement or eurythmics) are to be emphasized. Become sensitive to every harmony of tone or color. In creating art, strive to achieve the same kinds of rhythm and coördination which you observe among great artists. Note the swing and balance they have achieved. Practice until you secure similar results for yourself.

Participation in Group Activities. When studying music, you may learn a great deal by taking part in orchestras; other instrumental ensembles, choruses, glee clubs, and types of exhibits and performances may also be very useful. In the beginning, you may find it necessary to take minor parts in group work. Do not hesitate to assume a subordinate position. *Remember that the main purpose is to learn as much as possible from your participation.*

Specialization in One of the Arts. It is an excellent policy to get acquainted with several of the arts. At least, you should learn to appreciate the chief forms of art expression. Try, however, to specialize in one or two of the art subjects. Do your best both to appreciate and to create. In music, for instance, you may learn to enjoy the best productions, to perform on some favorite instrument or to sing, and to compose your own selections. Do not be misled by the superstition that some persons cannot learn; everyone who can learn to speak, can learn to appreciate music and perform it creditably, through one musical medium or another. Find the art you like best and in which you can attain most proficiency. The rest is careful practice and hard work. You may or may not become a first-class artist; but you will become a discriminating consumer and effective performer.

Value of Careful, Planned Practice. In fine arts, careless practice must be avoided. Be sure to practice in the right way, forming the correct habits, and changing your technique to achieve superior results. Follow instructions accurately; observe the methods used by skilled artists; do not imitate everything they do, but try to secure similar effects. Finally, schedule your practice time, and adhere faithfully to the schedule.

CHAPTER TWELVE

Study of
FOREIGN LANGUAGES

> "Apply each rule of grammar in speaking, reading, and writing. Memorize new words and idioms through use. Practice conversation. Learn to use French in life situations."—**F. M. du Mont**

Choice of a Foreign Language. For most purposes of a practical nature, you should carefully consider the advisability of studying at least two modern foreign languages, such as French, German, Italian, or Spanish. German is useful if you expect to do much scientific research. French is valuable in the study of the humanities and the social sciences. There are many families of languages, such as the following: Indo-European, Semitic, Hamitic, Ural-Altaic, Dravidian, Malay-Polynesian, Caucasian, Bantu. The Indo-European family includes Greek, Latin, Romance languages (French, Spanish, Portuguese, Italian, Rumanian, etc.), Teutonic languages (German, Dutch, English, Flemish, Scandinavian languages), Aryan, Armenian, Baltic (Lithuanian, Lettish, and Slavonic tongues), and Albanian. It is sometimes best to limit oneself to the study, at one time, of languages belonging to the same family.

Some educators are skeptical about the wisdom of devoting years of study to Latin or Greek. On the other hand, it is frequently asserted that study of the classical languages assists one's command of English. Unfortunately, few students acquire a working mastery of these languages. Those who condemn the study of Latin or Greek maintain that it would be best to spend the required time on the further study of English. These critics assert that most students quickly forget what they have learned of classical languages, never master them efficiently, and fail to secure benefits comparable to the great amount of work required. There are however, many worthwhile advantages to the study of ancient languages, especially if one can learn to think in terms of the language, and live with it. At any rate, you should read translations of the great classical masterpieces.

Acquisition of Feeling for a Language. What does it mean to have a feeling for a language? First of all, it means to be able to appreciate and use its rhythm, the swing of its phrases. Second, it means to be able to think in terms of the language, giving the words and phrases just the correct emphasis, and speed of delivery. It means also to be able to grasp the meanings of sentences as wholes, without having to dissect or analyze each word, and without translation. Last, feeling for a language involves the formation of many habits, so firmly fixed, through attentive repetition, that we express ourselves readily and spontaneously in speaking and in writing the language. The accent, swing, pitch, and tone qualities in speaking become habitual, as do also certain fine distinctions between oral and written expression in the language.

You can acquire a feeling for a language by listening to its rhythm and practicing its rhythm; by thinking in the language about daily affairs, other subjects you are studying, abstract ideas, etc.; by reading, listening to, and expressing complete sentences as wholes, not by trying to build sentences up word by word; and by using the language correctly, so often and in such a variety of contexts that you form set habits of expression.

If you acquire feeling for a language, mastery of its essentials will come to you easily. It will be a simple matter to enlarge your vocabulary, and you really will remember what you learn. Without this natural feeling, your study is bound to be laborious, and results less permanent and less effective.

Review of Other Subjects in a New Language. One of the best means to insure thinking in a new language is to review in that language what you have learned in history, literature, science, and other subjects. If you are studying French, why not think in French about the high spots of other subjects you are studying? Also talk and write, in French, about what you have learned of other subjects. You will find this practice one of the most successful methods of acquiring a real mastery of a foreign language.

Value of Thinking in a Foreign Language. Read a foreign language without too much reference to English. You may find this policy slow and difficult at first, but you will get results. When you do translate, try to re-state the material in the foreign language first, using your own words; then, you may translate it into English. In this way, you will make active use of the new language, without too many artificial relationships between the new language and English. The way to learn to use a language readily and correctly, is to use it in a natural, correct, rhythmic fashion. *You must think and feel in terms of the language you are studying.* In German, for instance, the words "Ich habe das Buch" should signify a special meaning at once, and should not have to be translated into "I have the book." In French, the sentence "Je suis un homme" should be a natural significant idea to you, without the need of translation into "I am a man." Translation is like a crutch; you never learn to use the language spontaneously if you rely too often on such an artificial aid while learning the language.

The Mastery of Grammar. Foreign languages should not be learned merely on the basis of grammar. Grammar should be a supplementary source of reference. Grammar explains why the language is used in the characteristic forms and particular constructions it assumes. Consult the hints supplied by your grammar; but be sure to apply these hints in repeated natural use of the language. It is possible to speak English well, without studying grammatical rules and the isolated constructions usually emphasized. Just as English grammar, however, helps you improve your English, by application in speaking, reading, and writing; so the grammar of a new language helps you master that language through similar application of grammatical principles.

Use of Familiar Subject-Matter. Another excellent method of learning a foreign tongue is to read material the content of which you already know. This method is unfortunately neglected in most schools and colleges, but has been found of the greatest value by individuals who wished to master a new language quickly and efficiently. If you know a story thoroughly, you will search for the meanings and ideas when you read it in a foreign language. If possible, make some use of a dictionary in the same foreign language. Sometimes you can use an all-French, or all-German, or all-Spanish dictionary, when reading in the respective foreign language. *Concentrate on the author's ideas and his message as a whole.* Use the "all-foreign" dictionary to verify meanings. When you get acquainted with a new word, apply it in writing, speaking, and thinking, in a variety of context, and always in the new language.

The Importance of Rhythm and Pronunciation. Acquisition of feeling for a language is helped by smooth, correct rhythm and the type of pronunciation characteristic of the language. Listen carefully to natives when they speak the language; listen to phonographs and radio lectures in the language; repeat what you hear. Ask for criticisms and corrections of your tone, accent, pronunciation, phrase rhythm, and expression. Note the many peculiarities of emphasis and delivery when you hear natives converse or read. Practice until you can secure the same distinctive results. Experiment with the position of your tongue and the action of lips, mouth, and glottis. Continue to practice until you secure the results you want. In silent reading, try to eliminate lip movements; try to grasp a whole sentence at a glance. Also, read orally, for the gist, without stopping to analyze individual words.

Value of Writing. Begin writing in simple terms, and use the "all-foreign" dictionary sometimes as a source of new words. If you cannot understand the definitions, you will then have to consult a bi-lingual dictionary. Use the same method when you want new or superior words in a foreign language. Write about all sorts of topics. Write about current events, other studies, personal affairs, sports, books, travel, music, art, and other interesting subjects. Ask natives to criticize your work. Read many well-written stories and essays in the foreign language; then re-write the same stories or ideas, in your own words, in the new language. Read and re-write business letters and excerpts from foreign newspapers.

Value of Conversing. If you can possibly do so, engage in frequent conversations with natives of the relevant foreign country. Try to restrict all discussion so that everyone will speak in the foreign language. Have dinner with friends who can speak the language well. Form or join a language club or group so that you will have constant opportunities to converse. Ask yourself questions and answer them, all in the language you are studying, e.g., "Ich habe das Buch." *"Was* habe ich?" "Ich habe *das Buch."* "Wer hat das Buch?" *"Ich* habe das Buch."

The Importance of Repetition. The president of one of the largest and most successful systems of language schools in the world has maintained that the average adult requires about thirty-five repetitions to master a new word with a fair degree of efficiency. This number of repetitions may not be necessary for some words, but others may need even more. *It is important to use a new word in connection with many different ideas.* Write the word in a sentence; say it in a sentence; read it in a sentence; think it in a sentence. Then, repeat the whole process many times. Do the same with idioms, and with whole phrases. You will soon develop an excellent working vocabulary.

Abundant Reading. We have suggested that you read familiar materials in the foreign language you are studying. Read also a variety of subject-matter: newspapers, periodicals, textbooks, fiction, essays, reference works, and poetry. Read for the gist of the material. Then write, in the foreign tongue, your reactions to what you have read. Skim through a great many essays and stories; then re-read them more carefully. As you read, avoid all reference to English. Also, read aloud from time to time. Listen to natives reading, and re-read aloud the same subject-matter you have heard them read.

No Single Method. Do not take seriously the advice of those who urge you to learn only to read or speak a foreign language. If you study correctly, you will learn to read, speak, and write proficiently. Conversation will help you read and write; writing and reading properly will help you speak. The wrong method of learning leads to a one-sided emphasis on reading to the neglect of oral expression. Insist on studying languages in a variety of ways, through constant reading, speaking, and writing.

Drawing can be used to great advantage in learning any foreign language. Note the following rough sketch drawn to show how easily French words can be mastered without use of English equivalents.

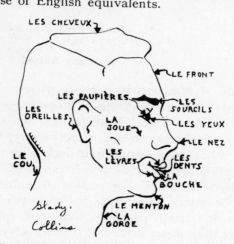

From brochure for *Thinking with a Pencil*, a forthcoming volume on visual education, by Henning Nelms.

Drawing such cartoons associates the foreign vocabulary with meaningful ideas or episodes. It tends to exclude any English translation so that the student can concentrate all his attention on the foreign language, and it provides practice in the natural use of the new vocabulary.

Of course, speaking, writing, and drawing will be worse than useless unless you think carefully about the language whenever you use it. Without careful thinking you can learn mistakes as easily as the correct expressions. There is no substitute for hard work.

CHAPTER THIRTEEN

Study of
MATHEMATICS

> "Mathematics takes us into the region of absolute necessity, to which not only the actual world, but every possible world, must conform."—Bertrand Russell

Nature of Mathematics. Mathematics is a science dealing with number and space processes — reality in its quantitative aspects. Branches of this science are arithmetic, algebra, geometry, trigonometry, differential and integral calculus. Arithmetic deals with the simpler number relations and problems of reasoning. Algebra is a condensed and modified extension of arithmetical reasoning. Geometry deals with the properties of space. Problems and relationships of plane and spherical triangles are the subject-matter of trigonometry. Differential calculus treats of the successive differences among the terms of a series of quantities; integral calculus deals with the reverse process, deducing magnitudes from changes in their series. There are also numerous other specialized fields of mathematics.

Choice of a Branch of Mathematics. Arithmetic is, of course, the most familiar field of mathematics. Algebra and geometry are also of considerable value in the study of the various sciences. The other more intricate subjects of mathematics are of less importance to the average citizen. Critics of these advanced subjects assert that probably almost all who have studied them have soon forgotten what they learned and have made little or no use of it, unless it be to teach the same material to others. Mathematics is indispensable in certain occupations, such as engineering research, navigation, and machine designing. We may assume, moreover, that a general knowledge of two or three branches of mathematics will sufficiently strengthen the average person's skill in dealing with problems of number, space relations, and business affairs. Unless, therefore, you can develop a special interest in the study of this science or anticipate a practical need for intensive mastery, limit yourself to arithmetic, and two or three selections from among algebra, geometry, trigonometry, and calculus.

Review of Arithmetic. Buy an inexpensive arithmetic fundamentals test, and test yourself on your mastery of fundamental processes (addition, subtraction, multiplication, division) and the use of certain common computations and measures (interest, metric weights, linear measures, etc.). Find your weaknesses and concentrate on drill work until you are sure of all processes. Construct and solve many problems requiring repeated use of the numerous terms and combinations.

Review also the various types of arithmetic problems. Improve your skill in quick analysis and solution of problems. Read a problem through rapidly first; then, analyze it so as to determine what is given, what is required, and the processes to use. *Form a habit of searching for the key to a problem, the decisive point to be cleared up or the precise element needed for its solution.* In solving problems, write down the important steps as you go along; in this way, you will avoid the necessity of retracing your work repeatedly whenever you come to a difficult part of the problem. Check all computations carefully. Verify the terms of your final answer by comparing with the factors called for in the problem. Apply your answer to all the parts of the problem, to be sure that all parts balance.

Construct a great many of your own problems similar to those in the textbooks, to insure sufficient review of the subject. Try to increase your speed of computation, making use of as many short cuts as possible. For example, suppose you wish to multiply two numbers such as 70171 and 69847. If you place 70171 below 69847 as follows $\frac{69847}{70171}$ you will need to multiply only by 1 and by 7. This procedure is of course much more efficient than placing the smaller figure, 69847, underneath, and multiplying 70171 by each of the figures in 69847. Analyze your figures before beginning to compute; then, use the short cuts.

Study of Algebra. When you are studying algebra, be sure to understand thoroughly every new concept and process. Practice until you are expert, before proceeding to the more difficult steps. The most important factor is the building of a good foundation. In dealing with algebraic problems, examine all facts carefully, determine the required points, and the equations most probably successful. In some cases, a difficult problem may be simplified by substituting numbers for symbols, or by estimating and experimenting with a probable answer. *Try to find the vital point, the key to the problem.* Bear in mind always every one of the facts given. If you are still unable to make progress, after considerable effort, consult similar problems in the text. At times, it may be advisable to take a rest, and begin afresh with the problem as a whole. It may also be helpful to assume an answer, and see how the facts of the problem would be related to each other when the assumed answer is introduced. Verify your final answer by fitting it into the problem so that all parts balance perfectly.

If you are careful to advance slowly from simpler to more difficult algebraic processes and problems, constructing and solving numerous exercises and problems of your own, similar to those in textbooks, you will have little cause for anxiety. With success, you will find that the subject will increase in attraction and become a highly interesting study. There is a certain intellectual pleasure in successful solution of puzzling or challenging problems.

Study of Geometry. Review frequently all axioms and first principles of geometry. Analyze all axioms, theorems, and problems with great care. Practice writing, *in your own words,* the various steps of each axiom, theorem, and problem. Be careful to study every one of the propositions and problems of your text; otherwise, you may later find yourself baffled and at a loss as to the cause of your difficulty. Draw all sorts of figures, numbers, angles, letters, and lines, to help you picture every step and point of a theorem or problem. Be sure you understand, and can apply every term, step, process, and principle.

Geometric Theorems (Propositions). Review the axioms and propositions you have previously studied. Analyze propositions to find: the facts given; the facts required; how each fact may best be illustrated; every step in the proof, and the reasons for every step. Be sure you understand every point; reason out each step; then review. outline, and analyze what you have learned.

Apply propositions by drawing your own figures, stating some of the dimensions, and requiring yourself to find others. Also, explain propositions in your own words; then write each step, revising your language to insure brevity, clarity, accuracy, and careful illustration of all steps. Finally, make up problems whose solutions require the application of the geometric theorems you are studying.

Occasionally, review the geometric terms with which you have worked, drawing figures to which you can apply the terms.

Use a code system to list the theorems you have studied. In this way, two or three words will represent a theorem. This procedure will help you review all theorems, and recall them when you need one of them to solve a problem.

Method of Solving Geometric Problems. Analyze the problems to determine the following: the facts given; the terms used, and the significance and meaning of each term; what is to be proved; possible connecting links between the answer and the facts given; the probable processes, axioms, and propositions involved.

Estimate the possible answers to a problem. Draw all figures carefully. Try to recall various propositions that might apply, and experiment with them, pushing every application until satisfied that it will or will not work. Draw a variety of helpful figures.

It is best to restrict yourself to problems not too far in advance of the theorems which you are sure you have mastered thoroughly. Try to find the key to a problem, the one point which, if proved, would solve the problem. Practice with many similar problems, without necessarily solving each one, but quickly finding the key principle or point involved.

If you meet with difficulty, persist. Try to find examples of similar problems in the textbook. Rest a while, and start all over again. Do not give up unless you know you have selected a problem far beyond your stage of progress. Review axioms and propositions, as well as difficult problems you have previously studied. It is best not to ask for help unless you feel that the situation is definitely hopeless. Once you have been assisted to solve a problem, however, construct many similar problems, and solve several of them from time to time, until you are positive you will not forget the relevant principles, illustrations, and processes. It is also excellent practice to try to solve problems in a variety of ways. Be sure to verify every solution and every step in the proof. You should have a good reason for choosing a particular line of attack. At each point make certain that what you have done is reasonable and consistent with familiar experience and with all the conditions stated in the problem. Ask yourself whether every result of your computations and equations is logical. Before doing the final computations, however, list all the theorems and equations which you plan to use in solving the problem. Finally, modify your language and ways of presenting a proof to make all steps in the solution brief, clear, logically placed in relation to other steps, and neat in appearance.

CHAPTER FOURTEEN

Study of
PHILOSOPHY,
RELIGION, PSYCHOLOGY

"What is the first business of one who studies philosophy? To part with self-conceit. For it is impossible for anyone to begin to learn what he thinks that he already knows."—**Epictetus**

Study of Philosophy. Philosophy presents the ideas of man about the world as a whole and about the fundamental problems of human life. Philosophy has various branches, such as metaphysics (dealing with the nature of reality or existence); logic (the laws and problems of thinking); ethics (problems of value and moral behavior); epistemology (investigation of how man acquires knowledge — theories of the nature and origin of knowledge); and aesthetics (the study of the appreciation and nature of beauty). Everyone should study philosophy; for everyone necessarily has some philosophy or view of the world and should benefit from the best thinking of mankind on this subject.

In general, there are two ways in which philosophy has been written and studied: the historical, or system-building; and the problem, or piece-meal. Study the subject in both ways. Consider the chronological development of philosophical systems as a whole, and of each major problem; also study problems as such, using historical references as sources of data and suggestions.

Re-state ideas in your own words. *Compare one idea with another, one system with another, one point of view with another. Study all sides of controversial questions.* The student of philosophy must have only one loyalty during his study of this subject, a loyalty to truth; and he must be prepared to follow all lines of reasoning to their ultimate conclusions.

Review often the ideas of which you are not quite sure. Review, from time to time, the high spots relating to a system or a problem of philosophy. Construct brief outlines, draw diagrams, criticize and make up your own mind, write your reactions. Consult encyclopedias, theses, journals, and other reference works. Refuse to be pessimistic, skeptical, or subject to one exaggerated mood. Problems in this field of knowledge may never be completely solved; all decisions are but tentative estimates based on the contemporary resources of individual minds; be philosophical about all moods and ideas. On the other hand you may, after due consideration, be justified in acquiring a feeling of certainty about fundamental conclusions in philosophy.

Study of Religion. It is no accident that the most noted scientists of all ages have been deeply religious. They, perhaps, even as much as specialists in religious education, have appreciated the limitations of human reason and the wonderful mystery of the universe.

Religion is concerned not merely with outward forms, rites and worship but especially with the fundamental beliefs and attitudes of the individual. Religion, while it necessarily involves the use of language and judgment, emphasizes faith and free choice of your view of human existence.

Most religions have certain basic considerations in common, such as: belief in a universal principle or Deity; respect for and observance of high ethical standards; a profound faith in the brotherhood of man and the value of human personality; and affirmative solutions to the perpetual problem of immortality.

You should participate in the religious experiences offered in educational institutions. Wholehearted interest in this field can hardly fail to benefit you, not only as a student but especially as a human being.

Study of Psychology.   Psychology has sometimes been defined as the science of mind and behavior. It deals mainly with purposive activity connected with emotions, thoughts, feelings, memory, habits, instincts, and the like. There are many schools of psychology, and the student should become well acquainted with the views of each school. For this reason, it is necessary to use a number of textbooks rather than only one. A good summary of many texts on psychology is contained in "An Outline of General Psychology."* A reading of this outline should indicate to you the general characteristics of the subject and the high desirability of studying it intensively.

Analyze and write about psychological laws and theories in your own words; then revise your summaries, using the terminology of the science. This procedure will go far to insure real understanding as well as retention of the subject-matter. Observe the operation of psychological laws and factors in the behavior of others.

Discuss psychological problems with other students; write your reactions to the views of each school of thought in connection with the major topics of the subject. Compare and contrast the ideas of various authors regarding disputed points.

Perhaps the most important test of sincere effort and learning, in this field, is the extent to which you practice the principles of the science. For example, you may read about the laws of readiness, exercise, and

---

* Published by Barnes and Noble, Inc., New York.

effect; if you understand their significance, you should use them as guides to your methods of studying, not only in this but also in other subjects. Construct notes and outlines; review them frequently; build new ideas on those you have previously learned; attempt only as much as you feel you will be able to accomplish. Consult encyclopedias, journals, theses, and other reference works.

CHAPTER FIFTEEN

Study of the
PHYSICAL
and
BIOLOGICAL SCIENCES

> "The scientific method is concerned with how things *do* happen, not how they *ought* to happen. Knowledge of the way things do happen, with no ifs, ands, or buts, allows us to deal more effectively with our environment."—Stuart Chase*

Science is the study of the environment, especially in its relation to man; in a broader sense, it is the search for verifiable truths about man and nature. Based on observation, logical reasoning, and experimentation, science has definite laws and principles verified by observation and experience. Everyone should know something of both the main content and the method of the chief sciences. You should become acquainted with *biology* (dealing chiefly with living things); *chemistry* (the study of the composition and molecular changes of substances); *physics* (treating of the laws common to different substances); *astronomy* (science of celestial bodies-sun, moons, planets, stars, etc.); and *geology* (physical history of the earth and man as disclosed by the study of rocks and fossils). You should probably make an intensive study of at least two of these sciences.

The field of engineering deserves special mention in view of the vital role of engineering sciences in modern society. If you are planning to become an engineer, you should master a number of subjects in mathematics,

---

* From *Tyranny of Words* by Stuart Chase. Used by permission of the publishers, Harcourt, Brace & Co., New York.

physics, and chemistry. Engineering drawing is an introductory course dealing with the graphic tools and methods used by all engineers. Descriptive geometry covers the mathematical problems related to engineering drawing. Other important courses include: statics, dealing with the laws of things at rest; dynamics, concerned with the laws of things in motion; strength of materials, treating the subject of resistance to stress; thermodynamics, the science studying the action of heat; electricity and electronics, subjects of first importance not only to the eletrical but also to the civil, mechanical, chemical, aeronautical, and architectural engineers.

Each science has developed certain general concepts and scientific principles. Make certain that you fully understand these generalizations. Concepts such as energy, force, inertia, gravity, relativity, oxidation, radio-activity, elements, compounds, atoms, molecules, and combustion should be mastered through reading, application in writing and discussion, and wherever possible, through observation and experiment.

The scientist defines his problem carefully; gathers data relating to the problem; forms reasonable hypotheses that might explain the facts and answer the problem; tries out his theories under controlled conditions; observes, records, and interprets the behavior of changing factors in his controlled situation; comes to a conclusion which is verified by application and logical proof, or else discarded. Attack all problems and experiments in science in this objective, scientific fashion.

The best way to learn to appreciate and understand scientific method is to practice it until it becomes habitual.

In many instances, it will be possible for you to learn through experiments. Seize every opportunity to do so, for there is no superior method of learning. Experiments require, however, adequate preparation, including a careful definition of the problem, study of all facts given, and systematic planning of each step. Read your text both before and after completing an experiment. Do the work neatly, quickly, and accurately, closely observing and recording facts, conditions, causes, and results. Know the reason for every action in the experiment, taking no step until you understand its purpose. When following a formula, grasp the meaning of each part of the formula, before application. Draw complete diagrams and pictures, whenever they seem useful.

In your study of biology, physics, or chemistry you will learn many facts and principles that can be useful in everyday affairs. Much that you will learn can be applied, for example, to problems of diet, ventilation, and other factors important for health.

Besides doing as much observing and experimenting as you can, do a great deal of "free" searching to find problems to solve. Investigate the numerous problems of industry, agriculture, etc., and their relation to the various sciences. Follow up each of these problems, making use of reference works and every opportunity to observe, read, discuss, and experiment.

Review your previous work in arithmetic, algebra and geometry. A common weakness of students, in studying the various sciences, is the need for adequate mastery of elementary mathematics. For example, in the study of beginning chemistry, a knowledge of fractions and percentages is assumed.

Keep a systematic, continuous record of your scientific experiments, readings, and principles, together with observations, reactions, and special reasons for every step or decision. Analyze the significance of every conclusion.

CHAPTER SIXTEEN

Study of the
SOCIAL SCIENCES

> "Social studies teaching is inadequate if
> young people do not form the habit of
> weighing values, and of choosing values to
> which they can hold in the midst of con-
> fusion and conflict—in short, if they do not
> build day by day a defensible philosophy
> of life."—John A. Hockett*

Social studies have to do with the facts, conditions, problems, and customs of groups of men, or human beings in their social relationships. The most important of the social studies are economics, government, history, geography, sociology, education, and anthropology.

Economics. Economics deals with the production, distribution, and consumption of wealth, and with the practical conditions of life. There are many schools of thought concerning problems of economics. Study all points of view, including the extremes of conservatism and radicalism. As in the case of the other social studies, be skeptical of authors who claim to have dis- covered uniform laws; consider such discoveries tenta- tive suppositions or theories. Even in the case of so- called basic ideas concerning prices, wages, demand and supply, diminishing returns, and the like, there are many conjectures, unknown and uncertain factors. Beware of

---

* From John A. Hockett's "Are the Social Studies Skill Subjects?" appearing
in SOCIAL EDUCATION, May 1938 issue. American Book Company, publishers.

accepting, without critical reflection and comparison among diverse schools, any particular point of view; get acquainted with them all.

Concentrate on practical applications of a theory. If you are analyzing a generalization or so-called law, try to see how it can be applied to explain economic conditions in various countries, industries, or localities. An excellent way to begin the study of a topic is to relate it to prevailing conditions or events, e.g., contemporary relations between labor and capital in a special field, or the movement of foreign trade, or the condition of large segments of an agricultural population. Statistical tables showing wages and hours of work, over a period of years, may be the best way to begin the study of business cycles. Base general statements on facts, and test them by reference to facts.

The drawing of diagrams, construction of outlines, and such original work as the keeping of a diary of economic events of the day will help you master this difficult field. Read a variety of newspapers and compare the differing ideas of financial editors as well as the frequently colored presentations of economic news. Write your own reactions to economic problems, doing your best to be fair to all sides of controversial points. Remember that in this subject, the one who is most cocksure he has discovered final laws and truths is likely to be the most in error. The careful student, understanding a variety of theories, sees also the difficulties in each of them and arrives at conclusions that are to him, at least, only tentative hypotheses. Be sure to consider the possible effects of human psychology, with its motives, habits, and emotions, as factors in the direction of economic forces. *Avoid jumping at conclusions, without sufficient factual evidence.* Often we witness students assuming that wealth, for instance, is always distributed inequitably, without thorough analysis of the meaning of wealth, the actual distribution prevailing, and the various conflicting theories concerning the economic worth of individuals or groups. On the other hand, it would be equally absurd to assume that wealth, in any particular system of society, is always equitably distributed.

Beware also of using terms of which you do not know the exact shade of meaning. In discussion with others, use terms in the same sense as they do; otherwise you can never exchange your real ideas. *Strive to find every atom of truth in the points of view of those with whom you discuss economic questions, so that you may improve your own conceptions.* Beware of such terms as "human nature," "individualism," "exploitation," and other expressions, the loose application of which indicates a closed mind, a mind no longer open to the light of evidence or to a change in convictions.

Government. Use both the historical and the problem approach in your study of government. Note the changing views on political questions, throughout the decades, and the changing conditions of life during such periods of history. Draw comparisons and contrasts between present and past problems of local and national government.

Too many students come to the study of this subject with rigidly fixed prejudices, whether these be partisan, nationalistic, internationalistic, or what not. The first effort should be to regard such pre-conceptions as subjective, provisional, emotionalized assumptions. In your study of government, hold nothing sacred, no person, no institution, no idea; judge each of these strictly on its merits, on its consequences to the welfare of mankind.

Study, therefore, many systems of government and many philosophies of government. Compare one with another, and the reasons advanced for one with the reasons and conditions relating to the other. Moreover, accept present institutions as only the starting point for your study; try to discover ways in which political practices are defective and can be improved.

Read more than one kind of newspaper, more than one kind of periodical, more than one kind of book; read the ideas of all sorts of reactionary, conservative, liberal, radical, and ultra-radical groups. No man owes loyalty to a mechanism of government, but only to that mechanism when it contributes to the progress of society and when it is based on truthful theory and consistent practice. Strive, therefore, to understand both the strength and the shortcomings of each form and practice of government. Observe political factors in operation; analyze the relationships between economic, partisan, and other forces determining the direction of local and national governments.

Do not hesitate to join movements to attain practical progress in government. *But be careful not to be taken in by fine-sounding ideas not based on facts and intensive study.*

When political events take place, trace their remote as well as their immediate causes. For example, international difficulties are never isolated from long-continued historical contacts and relationships, economic and social, among nations. Do your best to distinguish between fact and propaganda, and be always suspicious of data issuing from sources which are not free to tell the truth. The hand of the author who pictures glorious political institutions and practices may be controlled by motives of fear for personal safety, exaggerated patriotism, or greed; or his ideas may be based on only one side of the story, the other being concealed, overtly or otherwise. Assume that there are at least two fairly meritorious sides to every major political question on which men sincerely disagree. Read the views of foreign writers as well as those of your fellow citizens.

Relate your study of government to treatises on the philosophy of the state. You may be astonished to find that some of the ancient thinkers, such as Lao Tse, Plato, and Aristotle, proposed rather advanced views about the various systems of political control.

We should distinguish between theories of government, as outlined on paper, and practices of government, when theories are subjected to the limitations and diversions caused by practical conditions. Almost any theory of government can be made to look presentable on paper. But which ideas, institutions, and practices seem to work out in reality, and what are the decisive factors? This type of question is the kind you should be mainly concerned with, in your study of government. Contemporary situations should be the starting point for study of numerous political ideas and problems.

History. There is a great deal of prejudice in the writing of history. Historians approach historical events from their own point of view, selecting some events as important, others as unimportant; some findings as true, others as false; and they differ widely as to the causes and effects of historical events and movements. Although there is a considerable number of facts upon which all, or almost all, historians agree, it is necessary to study the past from the diverse points of view of many historians. It is, therefore, necessary to consult many textbooks and other sources of reference.

The important value of the study of history is attained when you grasp the significance of historical trends of a civilization or group and when you apply the lessons of such historical trends to current problems of society. *As you read and compare various versions of historical periods, then, ask yourself: What are the lessons to be drawn from these events? How have conditions changed since then?*

In what respect are conditions the same? How should we strive to meet similar problems of today, in the light of the experience of the past and in view of changing conditions?

If you concentrate on major movements and their chief causes and effects, you will be able to connect dates and other factual material with important trends. Consider the effects of geographic facts on the history of a people; the consequences of economic inventions and conditions; the work of educational and other social institutions; and the results of governmental policies. If you follow these suggestions you should, with the help of a limited amount of drill work, have little or no difficulty remembering the time sequence of events. Exact dates are generally of negligible importance.

In some cases, an effective way to study history is to begin with the present, and trace contemporary ideas, institutions, and events to their roots in the past. Perhaps you will find it best to study history both backward from the present, and forward from the past. In constructing outlines, be sure to discriminate among the more important vital factors of national life and the minor but spectacular incidents such as battles and personalities. The great forces of history relate to climate; resources; economic progress; mass reactions; political, labor, educational, and moral conditions; and the like.

Use printed outlines freely, as reference and review helps; but do a great deal of supplementary reading on the chief points of these outlines.* In the study of history, extensive reading of important works is probably the most vital single factor. Consult periodicals, newspapers, historical fiction, biographies, state documents, texts, and reference works. Make brief notes and write your reactions to major items.

---

* Topical references to standard textbooks, arranged in convenient bibliography tables, are included in the *College Outline Series*. With this device you may see at a glance a variety of specific references to each important phase of the subject.

Geography. Geographic concepts and facts ought to be mastered in their relations to the progress of civilization. Geography has to do with the physical conditions and resources available to man. Instead of studying merely the dry isolated items usually over-emphasized, consider every concept and fact in connection with its influence on human events and problems. Concepts such as crop rotation, irrigation, and water and electric power, are important determinants of our ways of living. Devote special attention to the values of products and the uses of geographic products and instruments. Compare and contrast the physical characteristics and resources of various localities and countries. Always stress economic and human relations. Discuss and write about the connections between geographic facts and current industrial and social conditions.

Sociology. This study deals with the principles underlying the development of human society, with the customs, institutions, conflicts, and problems of men considered in their group relationships. You should plan to secure at least a bird's-eye view of this highly important field of knowledge.

Here, as in the other social studies, there are many divergent schools of thought. Reading the diverse points of view about social problems and comparing one view with the others is a very effective method of studying sociology. You should summarize the chief points of agreement and disagreement, and state your own reactions.

Most of the textbooks in this field are imposing works, filled with masses of data about community and individual cases. It is advisable to construct an outline of major ideas, comparing your outline with an authoritative printed one. When you read descriptions of community problems or individual histories, associate these illustrations immediately with the chief concepts listed in your outlines. Verify your comprehension of the technical terms of sociology by explaining them in your own words and checking your explanations against the text. You will find there are many opportunities to read fascinating literature about the realistic problems of modern communities, problems, such as poverty, crime, law, government, war and peace, and race relations. Get acquainted with the professional journals in this field and with the helpful articles on various sociological topics in encyclopedias, such as the *Britannica* and *The Encyclopedia of Social Sciences*.

Do some sociological research of your own. Investigate the social conditions prevailing in your community, relate your facts to sociological principles, and write your reactions.

Education. Education is the study of the growth and training, as well as the concomitant social re-adjustment, of all persons, young and old alike. Every citizen should know the main facts about the values and functions of school systems, the problems of learning and teaching, and the opportunities of self-education. If you intend to become a teacher, you will, of course, study the various professional subjects more intensively. These subjects include: history of education, educational psychology, educational sociology, methods of teaching, tests and measurements, etc.

You should read widely in the history of education, as well as in the field of educational psychology. In fact, these subjects should be helpful to you, no matter what your field of specialization may be. Unfortunately, many of the theoretical branches of this study are filled with glittering generalizations, rather than facts and practices. Do your best to observe the self-education of children and of adults; connect your readings with the items you observe. If you have the chance, get some experience teaching other people some of the subjects you have mastered. Try out the principles of educational psychology and the ideals and experiments emphasized in the history of education.

Remember that education, in a realistic and correct sense, takes place in response to many experiences and is not limited to the activities of schools and school curricula. The educational influence of the press, the church, the business firm, the family, the theatre, and all other great agencies of society must be studied if you are truly to understand the problems and principles of education.

Anthropology. The science of anthropology investigates the natural history of man considered as a member of the animal kingdom. Anthropology traces back, so far as possible, the physical, mental, and other characteristics of man, his development and works. Distinguish between this science and ethnology which is only one branch of anthropology, the branch dealing with the racial relationships of human beings. Many other studies may properly be said to be aspects of anthropology, including sociology, ethics, anatomy, physiology, psychology, etc. Anthropology is thus a very broad subject, encompassing the whole field of human development.

This study is one of the finest you can choose. It should give you an opportunity to delve into a wide variety of challenging fields of knowledge. It is, if correctly studied, one of the most useful subjects for the attainment of cultural background, general information, and tolerant understanding of human nature.

CHAPTER SEVENTEEN

Interpretation of
VISUAL AIDS

"Vision is one of the chief gateways of educative experience. Visual aids increase the speed of learning and improve the quality of self-education. What our eyes perceive our minds, with due concentration, should quickly appreciate and long retain."

—Edward Fitzgerald

Visual aids, if properly used, can save you much time and effort, and enrich your education. We emphasize, however, the words, "if properly used." Any instrument that is improperly applied may be futile or even detrimental to the process of learning. With very little expenditure of time and effort, you can acquire essential skills in the use of visual materials. We suggest that you read and re-read the following discussion carefully until you are thoroughly familiar with the illustrations.*

MAPS

General Considerations. Common varieties of maps include: physical; political; economic; statistical; historical; and combination types. Maps may also be classified according to their structure as: wall maps; textbook maps; outline maps; road maps; "spotted" maps (on which the use of colored pins indicate facts); and so on.

The ability to read maps with ease, relating their contents to the topics being studied, is generally taken for granted. Yet even in the case of geographic maps,

---

* Visual aids applicable to specialized fields of knowledge are not included in this discussion. Such aids are generally self-explanatory. All illustrations reproduced in this chapter are from various books in the *College Outline Series*.

many students have failed to acquire adequate skills. Even the relative sizes and positions of the continents are consequently indefinitely or erroneously conceived, to say nothing of frequent misconceptions concerning political subdivisions and further refinements.

Without a reasonably accurate mental image of geographical locations, one can hardly do justice to the material of the daily newspaper. Skill in interpreting maps is of great importance when dealing with the large body of facts encountered in the study of the various fields of knowledge. For example, in history, if a sketch map accompanying your reading be concerned with the progress of a current war, or the site of a Federal power project, you should be able to visualize instantly and with a degree of accuracy the location of the places concerned as related to contiguous or neighboring places. If you feel that your knowledge of geography is deficient in matters pertaining to locations, lose no time in making an intensive review of the subject. A brief study of a globe and world atlas may be all that is required.

Any reliable atlas for students (*Goode's School Atlas* is excellent) contains a wealth of useful information in addition to the maps. You should study certain essential aids such as: descriptions of the various map projections and their particular merits and limitations; illustrations of differences in *scale;* comparisons of units of measurement; and pronouncing indexes and general information relating to astronomical geography. Mastery of these topics should provide you with a permanent key to most of the data contained in maps, which you are likely to need.

Map Scales. Since maps must be constructed much smaller in area than the places they are drawn to represent, one of the cartographer's first considerations, in drafting a map, is the selection of a *scale* best suited to the requirements and limitations of the specific case. In

other words, a unit of measure must be adopted which
will permit the draftsman to represent proportionately,
within the confines of a map, the measurements of the
area concerned. The problem is like that of designing
a building with a fifty-foot frontage, on a piece of trac-
ing linen that is, let us say, some fifty inches in width.
At the most, in such cases, the draftsman can make his
drawing but fifty inches wide. Hence, he may select
as his scale, one inch for every foot that the building is
to occupy. His scale then shows an inch measurement,
divided into twelve equal parts, to represent a foot.

Maps must of necessity be drawn to a scale very
much smaller than that used for a building plan. The
bar which appears on most maps, entitled *Scale of Miles*
or simply *Miles,* is a measuring device, similar to the
draftsman's scale, by which the reader may determine
distances between points on the map. The scale shows
the units of measure being used to delineate miles, hun-
dreds of miles, or, if it be a large scale map, parts of
a mile.

The smaller the area embraced by the map the larger
is the scale. Maps of cities are frequently drawn on a
scale large enough to show individual streets, public
buildings, parks, etc., in proper proportion. Students
who have formed the habit of using the scale will recall
that it is usually shown in the form of a fraction or proportion. Thus the scale "one inch to the mile," would
be expressed 1 :63,360 or 1/63,360 (since there are 63,360
inches to a mile). This is known as the R.F. or Representative Fraction. It means, simply, that every inch or

---

Fig. 6. At first sight this map appears to carry too much detail for its size;
it would probably repel many readers. On closer inspection, however, one is
surprised by the clearness with which the chief sovereign states are shown.
Undoubtedly the author did not intend that its entire contents should be assimi-
lated at once; much of the detail is serviceable as a convenient reference for the
text matter. Form the habit of studying such maps methodically, with the
objective of imprinting the essentials on the mind first, then going back for
the details.

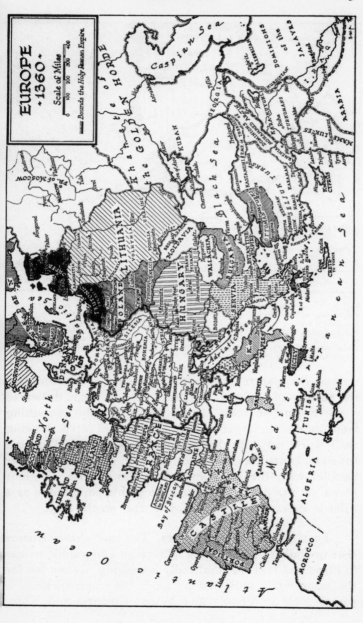

Fig. 6. (*See Note, Bottom of Page Opposite*).

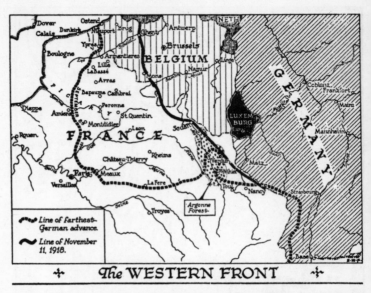

The WESTERN FRONT

Fig. 7. A sketch-map that is typical of many currently appearing in newspapers, magazines, and textbooks. For the discerning student who gives them more than a cursory glance, such maps often tell a highly significant story. Words alone fail to describe adequately the extent of Germany's penetration of France during World War I. Note how this map illustrates the dramatic nearness with which the Central Powers came to occupying the French capital itself. What places shown were the locations of major battles?

unit on the map represents 63,360 inches or like units on the surface of the earth. Atlases present maps drawn to a much smaller scale than 1:63,360, rarely containing maps on a scale larger than 1:500,000, and often showing their world maps on the scale of 1:100,000,000. The next time you consult a map, place the edge of a piece of paper parallel with the scale and mark the various divisions given, on the paper. Practice using this paper edge as a ruler in determining various distances on the map.

Foreign Geographic Names. The lack of consistency that prevails in the spelling of foreign geographic names in maps and texts is admittedly confusing. When we see the same cities indicated by more than one spelling or name, such as Vienna and Wien; Cologne and Köln;

FIG. 8. In studying such maps as this and the preceding example, note first the title, then look for the legend or key giving the meanings of special marks and shadings. In this case we find the legend directly beneath the title. After careful examination of this map you should be able to visualize the geographical location of the various territories lost (the blackened areas) such as, Alsace and Lorraine in the *south-western* corner of Germany; the portion of Upper Silesia in the *middle-eastern* section; the large, vital area to the *north-east*, which separates East Prussia from the mother country, thus creating the controversial *Polish Corridor;* and the *Saar* area.

Munich and München; Reval, Revel and Tallinn; Dorpat, Jurjev and Tartu; to mention but a few, we have good reason for our vexation and confusion. Were the student familiar, however, with the virtually insurmountable difficulties encountered in the attainment of absolute consistency, he would then understand the reasons for this seemingly deliberate attempt to baffle him.

It can only be recommended here that you accept this extra burden philosophically; make inquiry and research concerning the form now acceptable to the best authorities; and meanwhile take encouragement in the knowledge that in the interests of consistency, the use of local official names (names of countries excepted) is now being favored by the United States Government, the various Geographical Societies, and the largest

American publishers of maps and atlases. It may be discouraging for us to have to think of such celebrated old friends as Naples, Vienna, Lemberg and Cologne by their odd-sounding native names of Napoli, Wien, Lwów and Köln, but undoubtedly it is all for the best.

GRAPHS

As a rule, tables of numerical data, particularly when they are long and complex, are not the most satisfactory means of conveying statistical information. Aside from appearing uninteresting in themselves, their very nature often permits important facts to remain unnoticed. To overcome the undesirable features of tables and lists of comparative data, we use the graph. The chief function of the graph is to present statistical matter in visual form, thus permitting comparisons to be made quickly and clearly.

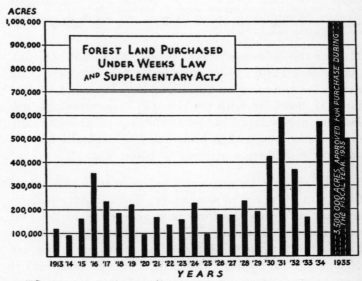

FIG. 9. The bar chart. The enormous increase in purchases during 1935 necessitated the combining of four bars in this case. Another alternative would have been the showing of a "break" in one bar, supplemented by the figures concerned.

The objective here is merely to introduce those types of graphs most frequently met in the student's reading, with a view to encourage their use in his own work. Since this form of visual aid is employed as a matter of course in industry and business as well as in school and college, the little effort required to master and memorize the various types illustrated, will be well expended by the student. To those wishing a more complete presentation, a text on graphs is recommended.

The Bar Chart. The bar chart is so simple as to be self-explanatory. Although the thickness of the bars remains constant, the lengths vary in proportion to the amounts being represented (see Figures 9, 11). The bars may be placed either horizontally or vertically.

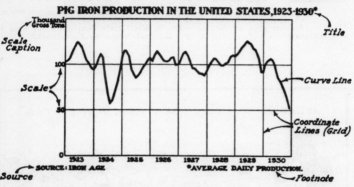

Fig. 10. Time series type of line graph. Labels have been introduced into this example to point out component parts of its structure.

The Line Graph. The line graph, illustrated in Figure 10, is one of the most commonly used types of graph. Here we see that variations are expressed by a line, known as the *curve line*, which varies in its distance from the base line. The course of this line is often simplified by the introduction of a *freehand line*, which expresses the trend. The line graph is generally preferred when there is considerable data to be correlated.

PROPORTION OF RURAL AND URBAN POPULATION
IN UNITED STATES, GREAT BRITAIN, GERMANY AND FRANCE

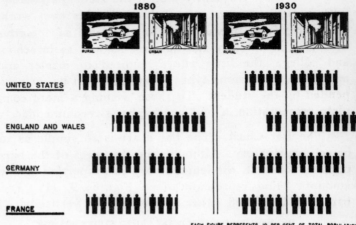

EACH FIGURE REPRESENTS 10 PER CENT OF TOTAL POPULATION

FIG. 11. Another type of the bar chart, in which individual units are used to compare quantities. (From *Our Cities*, National Resources Committee).

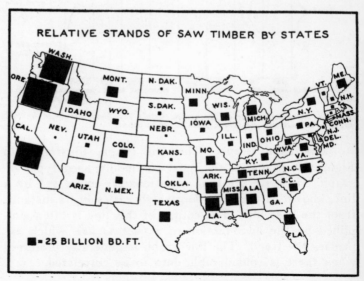

FIG. 12. Area map diagram.

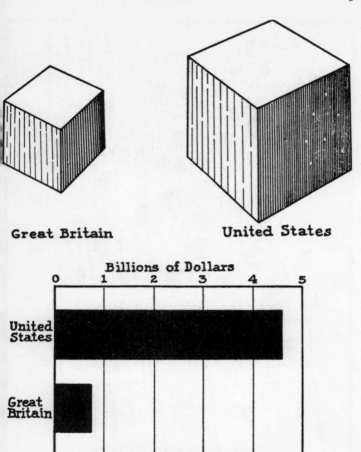

Great Britain   **United States**

FIG. 13. The same data made visual in solid diagram (above) and in bar chart form for comparison.

Solid and Area Diagrams. Diagrams that contrast area and volume are very much like the bar chart, excepting that the quantities contrasted are proportional in *area* or *size* to the quantities they represent instead of being proportionate in length. Figure 13 clearly shows a comparison of the bar chart and solid diagram in convey-

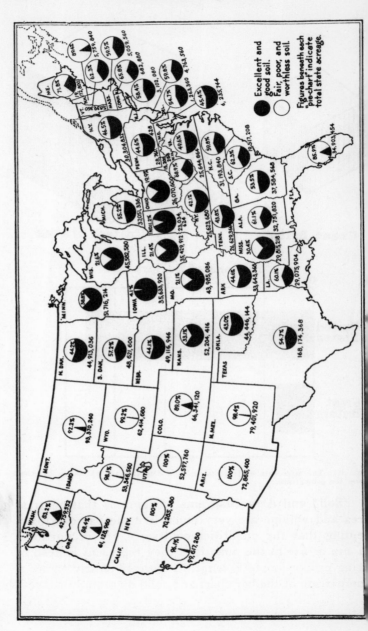

ing the same information. Note that the solid diagram is
inferior to the bar chart, since it is more difficult to
estimate the value of the two figures being compared.

Either of these types of illustration may assume a
variety of shapes. The familiar cartoon comparing
human beings of different sizes falls into the category of

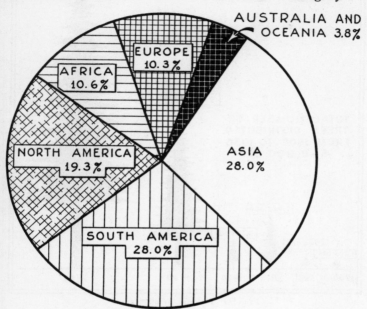

FIG. 15. Pie chart, in which shading has been used to aid in distinguishing the
various segments.

the pictorial solid diagram. The pie chart, Figures 14, 15,
is a form of the area diagram, in which the circum-
ference of the circle represents 100 per cent. The segments showing the different quantities compared are
often given contrasting shading to aid in distinction.

Organization and Line-of-Flow Charts. In describing intricate organizations, such as the Federal Govern-

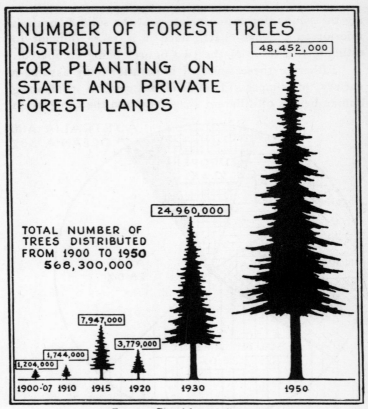

NUMBER OF FOREST TREES
DISTRIBUTED
FOR PLANTING ON
STATE AND PRIVATE
FOREST LANDS

48,452,000

24,960,000

TOTAL NUMBER OF
TREES DISTRIBUTED
FROM 1900 TO 1950
568,300,000

7,947,000

3,779,000

1,744,000

1,204,000

1900-07 1910 1915 1920 1930 1950

Fig. 16. Pictorial area diagram.

ment or one of its departments, or in setting forth the
hands through which a function passes, authors often
use what is known as organization and line-of-flow
charts. These charts save a great deal of time and effort
for the student who studies them with care.

Conclusion. This chapter has presented only a few
general hints concerning the proper uses of visual aids.
The value of such aids will depend upon your conscientious effort to get the most out of what you read.

It is important to remember that maps and graphs
are included by authors to simplify or clarify ideas, and

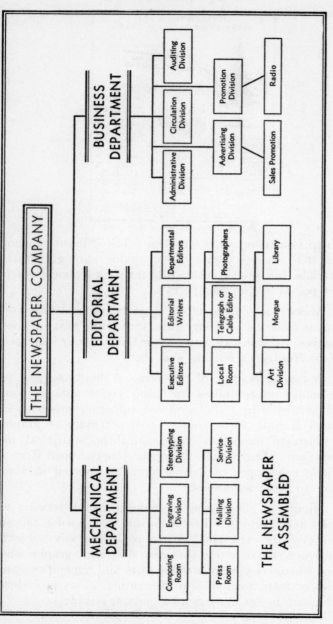

Fig. 17. Organization chart.

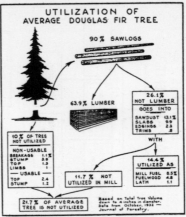

FIG. 18.   Pictorial line-of-flow chart.

to help you to retain those ideas. The efficient student does not merely glance at or skim through visual materials, but studies them diligently and reviews their chief points in his "mind's eye."

Make it a rule, therefore, to analyze visual aids, and develop methods of using them that work best in your situation. In this way, you cannot fail to derive increased benefit from your reading and study.

A careful reading of this chapter should suggest to you many opportunities for using visual aids in your own writing. In a thesis on contemporary problems in central Europe, for example, construct maps or graphs to illustrate important geographical or statistical information. Many times, a map or chart clipped from a reliable newspaper or journal may be inserted in your paper to great advantage.

Figure 20 shows how to make a useful drawing to clarify text material. Practice using such visual aids in your everyday studying and in reviewing any subject. Construct charts, crude sketches, diagrams, graphs, and maps whenever you wish to organize and remember principles or facts amenable to illustration. This procedure will insure better mastery of almost any subject.

FIG. 19. Line-or-flow chart.

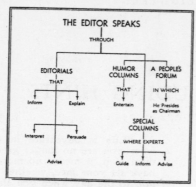

FIG. 20. How verbal statements are clarified by making drawings. (Contributed by Henning Nelms, from *Thinking with a Pencil* (in preparation).

The following text appears within the map drawing (Pl. 27):

Mediterranean Sea Pl. 27

This map is crude, but it is much easier to understand and remember than any description in words.

DESCRIPTION IN BOOK ON EGYPT
"From the first cataract, the Nile flows northward to Memphis, which marks the boundary between Upper and Lower Egypt. There, the river divides into the many mouths that run through the Delta to the Mediterranean."

When some new geographical fact appears in the book, we can easily add it to our map.

LATER PASSAGES
". . . built Alexandria at the most westerly mouth of the Nile."
"The Fayyum is a lake roughly thirty miles southwest of Memphis."
"The Nile makes a loop to the east just below the ruins of Karnak."

Drawing is also of great value in visualizing abstract ideas.

$(a+b)^2 = a^2 + 2ab + b^2$

CHAPTER EIGHTEEN

CONCLUDING HINTS

> "Life is adventure in experience, and when you are no longer greedy for the last drop of it, it means no more than that you have set your face, whether you know it or not, to the day when you shall depart without a backward look. Those who look backward longingly to the end die young, at whatever age.—Donald C. Peattie*

Necessity of a Well-Planned Program. As soon as possible, develop a tentative program of study. This program should be based upon:

1. Acquaintance with the main elements of many subjects,

2. Analysis of the vocational and practical values of the various subjects,

3. Consultation with friends and teachers, whose judgment you respect,

4. Consideration of your previous successes and difficulties in studying certain fields of knowledge, e.g., foreign languages, sciences, etc., and

5. Analysis of proper balance of emphasis among diverse kinds of activity; study, group associations, recreation, and rest.

---

* From *An Almanac for Moderns* by Donald G. Peattie. Used by permission of the publishers, G. P. Putnam's Sons, New York.

Programs of study should not be changed without sufficient reason; but do not hesitate to make changes justified by due consideration of your requirements.

Data about Teachers. Learn salient facts about your instructors. Who are the most popular, and why? Who are probably the most skillful? With whom will you benefit most from association? Analysis of these points may help you determine the best ways in which to get the most out of the services of your instructors. Observe your teachers carefully, and ask others for their opinions. Get whatever help you can even from teachers who restrict their class work largely to formal questions, recitations, drill work, etc.; but show a preference, if you are permitted to do so, for those who use a variety of effective methods of teaching. Frequently, when you are in doubt as to whether to study a subject during a particular year, consideration of the personality of the teacher may help you decide. Remember, however, that "snap" courses and easy-going teachers are of less service to you than courses and teachers that require high standards of work.

Rules and Regulations. Review with due care all requirements and regulations of the institution in which you are studying. What are the rules relating to use of the library, registration, examinations, residence, absences, grades, promotion, holidays, degree requirements, credits, matriculation, transfer of credits, fee payments, clubs and societies, location of instructional rooms and buildings, and the annual calendar? Show that you understand the serious aims of the institution, that you can cooperate with others, and that you are prepared to fulfill all requirements. If there are regulations you do not fully grasp, or if you meet with difficulty, do not hesitate to consult persons in authority. It is their business to help you, if properly requested.

The maintenance of a good record as to your studies and character is of the greatest importance. Strive for knowledge and skill, first and foremost; but remember that a good record testifies that others, in authority, are ready to vouch that you have been conscientious and successful. If you receive low ratings at any time, insist on learning the reasons, and promptly take measures to correct your weak spots.

Use of Available Resources. Make liberal use of all available facilities and opportunities, for example, libraries, excursions, special lectures and discussions, gymnasia, house privileges, clubs, institutional equipment and supplies, employment and personnel services, educational counseling. Too often, students are unaware of the fine equipment and opportunities of their institutions and communities.

Arrangement of Proper Conditions for Studying. The extent of your success in studying will depend in considerable measure on the conditions under which you do your work. You have been told often enough that you should take care of your eyesight, for instance, or that the light should come over your left shoulder. Such advice as the latter is not strictly correct, as it makes no difference from which direction the light strikes a page; the main point is to see that there is no shadow on the page, that you can see readily, without facing a glare, and that you are not straining your eyes. So, too, in respect to ventilation, quietness, availability of supplies, proper exercise and food, sleep and rest, recreation and regularity, and all the other admonitions of educational experts. Merely use your common sense, adjusting your practice to secure the best results. To increase the likelihood of success, criticize the conditions under which you study, and use the most hygienic, economical, and efficient methods. *If you are alert to what* *is happening, if you consider your handicaps and advantages, you will probably know your needs much better than anyone else does.* Devise a systematic schedule suited to your requirements, and follow it, being, however, willing to change for sufficient reason.

The Optimistic Attitude. Be optimistic. Refuse to permit yourself to drift into undesirable moods of fear or pessimism. Do not worry about examinations. Education is not the pocketing of so many units of subject-matter; it is growth in appreciation, understanding, wisdom, and character, more than it is anything else. Just do your best, and make the best of it. Accept difficulties as challenges. Learn from mistakes you make, especially the mistakes you try to avoid but seemingly cannot.

Choice of a Career. In planning your studies and your vocational career, consider the possibility of studying certain highly useful, practical subjects such as typewriting, shorthand, public speaking, and English composition. No matter what occupation or studies you choose, these subjects, effectively mastered, will prove of immense value to you.

You must not only prepare to earn a living; you must also live a life. Get the best cultural background you can, bearing in mind, however, that occupational studies may go far toward extending your cultural horizon, just as so-called cultural studies may greatly increase your vocational efficiency.

Consider the conditions and requirements relating to occupations in which you may become interested. Consult friends and vocational counselors; read guidance treatises; visit centers of the occupations and institutions that prepare for them; and discuss the occupation with its practitioners. If you can choose the type of work you like best, you will probably be happier and more efficient than you would be if restricted to less interesting work.

Having made up your mind as to a vocational choice, arrange your program of studies in accordance with the requirements of the vocation as well as your cultural needs. Specialize in the one field of concentration most useful for your anticipated vocational career. If you remain in doubt about an occupational choice, continue to study the opportunities and characteristics of the chief occupations until you can reach a decision. Do not hesitate to change your field of specialization at any time, when convinced of the wisdom of such changes. Perhaps your first selection should be turned into a hobby rather than a vocation for you to follow. Always consider that taking pleasure in one's work is the important factor, but have in mind the possibility of practical, financial success.

Financial Problems. In many cases, students encounter the unfortunate situation of financial difficulty in seeking to advance their education. Society has not yet wisely appreciated the importance of the very best education of youth and the very best training of its workers. If you must work your own way and find it difficult to do so, take a smaller program rather than sacrifice the quality of your studying. Do less and do it well.

If you must borrow, do so with the greatest conservatism and discretion. It may be far better to arrange terms with the educational institution in which you study than to plunge into private debts. Apply for scholarships in many institutions, not just one; you should have your chance to succeed. Apply at an early date for scholarships and part-time employment; applications may later be useless so far as your immediate financial needs are concerned. You will, of course, economize, buying used copies of texts (be sure they are the proper editions and complete); inexpensive printed outlines and use of the library may help you a great deal.

Do some real shopping before you spend your money. Few indeed are the salesmen who will explain the deficiencies of their products; they present only the bright side. You must learn to be a cautious, practical consumer. Hints on how to conserve limited funds have been ably summarized by C. C. Crawford.

"Compare relative values of articles before you purchase. Buy necessities first, and educational or school necessities first of all. Don't economize by doing without books, tools, and needed school equipment. It is false economy to do so. Get good quality of goods, even though it costs more; it pays in the end. Ask the price before buying, whether you are buying goods or membership in organizations. Pay your fixed charges, such as room and board, in advance. Buy a reasonable supply of recreation; it is a necessity. Don't run with the rich crowd—you won't be able to keep up. Be honest and admit poverty, instead of going under false pretenses. Remember where the funds you are spending have come from. Don't raise your standard of living unless you are sure you can keep it up, because it is very hard to go back to a lower standard when once you are accustomed to the higher one. Keep busy, and you will not spend so much. Avoid unnecessary habits of spending, such as eating between meals, and treating your friends. Always keep an emergency reserve on hand; and if you have funds above the needs of the current month, keep them in the savings bank where they will be free from your check, and where they will earn a small amount of interest.

"There are some specific suggestions for reducing the expenses of college life which may be worth considering at this point. Patronize second-hand book exchanges. Take good care of books so that they will bring good second-hand prices. Be careful with your books, pens, and supplies, to avoid losing them. Secure a locker at the university in which to keep your property in order to avoid loss or theft. Repair things before they are ruined. 'A stitch in time saves nine.' Buy paper by the ream instead of by the tablet. Buy ink in a large-size bottle that will last you all the year. Use one loose-leaf notebook for all of your courses. Have plain, unruled paper cut up into 3 by 5 cards, instead of buying stiff cards at the book store. Use these cards for scratch purposes, instead of wasting large sheets. Use an eversharp pencil instead of the old-fashioned wooden ones. Use fountain pen and ink wherever possible in preference to pencil. Avoid waste, whatever its form and magnitude."*

Conclusion. The student who conscientiously does his best is almost sure to succeed. Even if he does not achieve distinction, he will know that so far as he is concerned, he has grown in knowledge, power, and understanding. Remember that merely attending classes offers no guarantee that you will benefit as much as you should from educational opportunities. The process of self-education is endless.

---

* From *Methods of Study* by C. C. Crawford. Used by permission of the Author.

BIBLIOGRAPHY

Arkin, H., and Colton, R. R., *Tables for Statisticians*. New York: Barnes & Noble, Inc., 1950. A selection of 25 most frequently used tables (squares, square roots, cubes, cube roots, logarithms, reciprocals, factorials, areas of the normal curve, *t*, *F*, Chi Square, etc.) with clearly written instructions for the use of each table.

Bennett, M. E., *College and Life: Problems of Self-Discovery and Self-Direction*. New York: McGraw-Hill Book Company, 1952. 4th ed. A comprehensive discussion of college students' problems, with many specific suggestions on how to solve them.

Brittain, R., *Punctuation: A Practical Method Based on Meaning*. New York: Barnes & Noble, Inc. 1950. This study guide explains how to punctuate by reference to meanings instead of rules. Most of this information can be absorbed from a single reading of the text.

Chapman, S., *How to Study Physics*. Cambridge, Mass.: Addison-Wesley Press, Inc., 1953. A valuable pamphlet ,which includes suggestions on laboratory experiments, the study of mathematics, and the solving of science problems.

Cordasco, F., and Gatner, E. M., *Research and Report Writing*. New York: Barnes & Noble, Inc., 1955. 3rd ed. A comprehensive guide to research techniques, including bibliographies, including bibliographies and specimen papers.

Curme, G. O., *English Grammar*. New York: Barnes & Noble, Inc., 1947. One of the most authoritative and comprehensive summaries of English grammar ever published in a single volume. The book covers many topics not treated sufficiently elsewhere.

Dadourian, H. M., *How to Study, How to Solve: An Aid to Students of Mathematical Sciences*. Cambridge, Mass.: Addison-Wesley Press, Inc., 1951. A summary of effective methods of studying mathematics, with emphasis on problem solving, and many specific suggestions.

Frederick, R. W., Kitchen, P. C., and McElwee, A. R., *A Guide to College Study*. New York: Appleton-Century-Crofts, Inc., 1947. An extremely practical book for college freshmen which summarizes the main findings of the psychology of learning. There are valuable chapters on reading, observing, recording, writing and speaking.

Jenkinson, B. L., *Bureau of the Census Manual of Tabular Presentation*. Washington, D. C.: Government Printing Office, 1949. A highly detailed, practical analysis of the construction and interpretation of statistical tables. An invaluable referencee for the student.

Lutz, R. R., *Graphic Presentation Simplified*. New York: Funk & Wagnalls Co., 1949. A clear explanation of how to present facts in the form of charts, including curve, bar, circle, sector, and statistical map charts, and dot, pin and tack, and flow maps. There is a chapter on statistical procedures, and one on the construction of tables.

National Society for the Study of Education, *Reading in High School and College*. Chicago: University of Chicago Press, 1948. Part II of *the Forty-Seventh Yearbook,* edited by Nelson B. Henry. A. summary of problems, techniques, and suggestions for the improvement of reading.

Shepherd, W. R., *Historical Atlas*. New York: Barnes & Noble, Inc., 1956. The 8th revised edition of an excellent, standard reference work in world history.

Shores, L., *Basic Reference Sources*. Chicago: American Library Association, 1953. A valuable introduction, based on some 300 titles in various fields of knowledge, showing how to evaluate and use reference materials.

Sloan, H. S., and Zurcher, A. J., *A Dictionary of Economics*. New York: Barnes & Noble, Inc., 1953. Definitions are given for 2,800 terms from economic history, economic theory, international trade, finance, exchange, taxation, money, credit, and banking.

Smith, E. C., and Zurcher, A. J., *Dictionary of American Politics*. New York: Barnes & Noble, Inc., 1955. Provides definitions of more than 3,500 terms used in the study of American government and politics.

Webster's Biographical Dictionary, A Dictionary of Names of Noteworthy Persons with Pronunciations and Concise Biographies. Springfield Mass.: G. & C. Merriam, Inc., 1956. A reliable source of biographical information, including 40,000 historical and contemporary names.

Webster's Geographical Dictionary, A Dictionary of Names of Places with Geographical and Historical Information and Pronunciations. Springfield, Mass.: G. & C. Merriam, Inc., 1955. Provides quick-reference information about more than 40,000 places in all parts of the world together with 177 maps. Also included are 126 excellent statistical tables presenting data about mountains, national parks, power dams, and national mounuments.

Winchell, C. M., *Guide to Reference Books*. Chicago: American Library Association, 1951. 7th ed. Supplements, 1950–1952 (1954); 1953–1955 (1956). A dependable list of references about periodicals and newspapers, essays and general literature, debates, dissertations, encyclopedias, dictionaries, philosophy, religion, social sciences, science, useful arts, fine arts, literature, biography, geography, history, governmental documents, and bibliographies.

Index